Welcome

STIG ABELL
EDITOR, *TLS*

It is a verity generally recognized that a book in possession of a good Austen theme must be in want of a reference to the beginning of *Pride and Prejudice*. Jane Austen belongs to that small pantheon of great writers who remain both effortlessly fresh and engaging, while still being endlessly subject to pastiche. There are zombie versions of Austen novels, there are – it pains me to inform you – pornographic versions of her novels; indeed, it is hard to conceive of another great author (not Charles Dickens, not George Eliot, not Henry James) capable of sustaining such a broad response.

Part of the reason is apparent in the quality of the writing, the acuity of the vision, the universality of the themes: money, pride, love, disappointment, expectation, the confinement of our chance existence. There is also the fact that the brilliance of her output was never allowed to be obscured – as in the case of so many writers – by an indulgent late period or an experimental middle phase. No: she wrote six beautiful, important novels, published in a period of seven years, the last, *Persuasion* (1818), arguably even better than the first, *Sense and Sensibility* (1811). There are no duds, no excrescences, no failures.

When reading Jane Austen, there is a sense of completeness of vision, to match the completeness of her canon. The Oxford philosopher Gilbert Ryle was once asked whether he ever read novels; "Yes", he asserted, "all six, every year". His reaction is representative of many: Austen will always have her fervent votaries, her impassioned supporters. Ask your friends to rank the six novels in order of preference, and you will guarantee yourself a pleasing half-hour of robust fireside debate, just as if you were happily ensconced at Pemberley or Hartfield. And to help the debate, we hope you enjoy this collection of the *TLS*'s best writing about this wonderful writer, taken from the past hundred years.

My order, by the way, from most to least favourite, is: *Pride and Prejudice*; *Persuasion*; *Sense and Sensibility*; *Emma*; *Mansfield Park*; and *Northanger Abbey*. It's harder than it looks, you know.

Contents

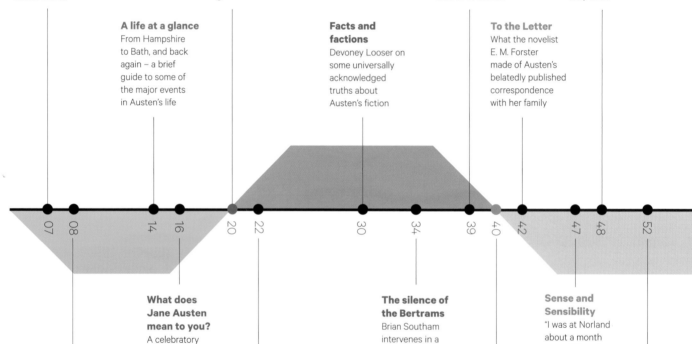

Plainly Jane
Watercolour, oil painting or waxwork? The controversial portraits of an elusive novelist

Wives and daughters
Claire Tomalin on the possibilities of women's lives in the eighteenth and nineteenth centuries

Praise and pewter
Claudia L. Johnson charts the novelist's gradual rise from obscurity to her present fame

Persuasion
"That is not good company, that is the best . . ."
An encounter in Bath, from Jane Austen's last novel

Keeping it in the family
Kathryn Sutherland traces the ways in which a literary legacy was guarded and fought over

The Times
A glance around Austen's Regency world, taking in family homes, battlefields and backstreets

Pride and Prejudice
"Mr Darcy soon drew the attention of the room . . ."
Making a first impression

What would Jane do?
Paula Marantz Cohen attends a happy gathering of fervent Janeites in Chicago

54 56 61 62 64 66 68 72 76 79 80 82 84 94 96 98

The Life
Portraits of the writer as, variously, a family heirloom, a young woman with a parasol and a literary spinster

Niece work
Kathryn Sutherland on *Miss Austen Regrets*, an impressively subtle biopic about the novelist

These conflicting times
The total war of Austen's age, according to Sudhir Hazareesingh

Austen adapted
The widely varying approaches to putting Austen's novels on screen – from Hollywood to Bollywood

Emma
"It was a sweet view – sweet to the eye and the mind . . ."
An approving view of an especially English rural scene

Sex and the Georgian city
Stella Tillyard explores London's elegant facades – and seedier backstreets

The Afterlife
A short history of Austen-inspired films, literary rewrites and gatherings of Austen aficionados

Ostensibly Austen
How novelists such as Helen Fielding and P. D. James, have reworked Austen's novels

Credits

Editor
Stig Abell

Issue editor
Michael Caines

Creative director
Darren Smith

Art director
Sachini Imbuldeniya

Design
Graham Smith

Sub-editors
George Berridge
Lucy Dallas
Samuel Graydon
David Horspool
Andrew Irwin
Alan Jenkins
Thea Lenarduzzi
Catharine Morris
Mika Ross-Southall
Adrian Tahourdin

Picture research
Matthew Glynn
Kara Messina

Editorial assistants
Lamorna Ash
Jennifer Hahn
Camille Ralphs
Clare Saxby

Illustrators
Darren Smith
Valentina Verc
Dan Neather
Simon Jugovic Fink
Martin Haake

With thanks to
Repro services
publishing operations

TLS

Contributors

Melvyn Bragg is a novelist and broadcaster, who presents the long-running *South Bank Show* and *In Our Time*. His books include *The Adventure of English* (2003) and *Now Is the Time* (2015).

Paula Byrne's books include *The Real Jane Austen: A life in small things* (2013) and *The Genius of Jane Austen: Her love of theatre and why she is a hit in Hollywood* (2017).

Amit Chaudhuri is a writer whose books include the novel *Freedom Song* (1998) and the anthology *The Picador Book of Modern Indian Literature* (2001).

Paula Marantz Cohen is Professor of English at Drexel University, Pennsylvania, and the author of novels such as *Jane Austen in Boca* (2002).

Robert Douglas-Fairhurst is Professor of English at Magdalen College, Oxford. His books include *Becoming Dickens: The invention of a novelist* (2011).

Lindsay Duguid is former fiction editor of the *TLS*.

Geoff Dyer is a writer whose books includes *The Ongoing Moment* (2005) and *White Sands: Experiences from the outside world* (2016).

Samantha Ellis is a playwright and the author of *How To Be a Heroine* (2014) and *Take Courage: Anne Brontë and the art of life* (2017).

E. M. Forster (1879–1970) was a highly distinguished writer best known for his popular novels, such as *A Room with a View* (1908), *Howards End* (1910) and *A Passage to India* (1924).

Tessa Hadley is an award-winning novelist whose books include *Accidents in the Home* (2002) and *The Past* (2015).

Jocelyn Harris is Emeritus

Professor of the University of Otago. Her books include *A Revolution Almost Beyond Expression: Jane Austen's Persuasion* (2007).

Sudhir Hazareesingh is a Fellow at Balliol College, Oxford, and the author of books such as *The Legend of Napoleon* (2004) and *How the French Think: An affectionate portrait of an intellectual people* (2015).

Mick Imlah (1956–2009) was poetry editor of the *TLS*. His second full collection of poems, *The Lost Leader* (2008), won the Forward Prize for Best Collection.

Claudia L. Johnson is Professor of English Literature at Princeton University. Her books include *Jane Austen's Cults and Cultures* (2012).

Devoney Looser is Professor of English at Arizona State University and the author of *The Making of Jane Austen* (2017).

Arthur McDowall (1878–1933), who had been both a leader writer for *The Times* and a Fellow of All Souls, Oxford, wrote hundreds of reviews for the *TLS*, championing Virginia Woolf and D. H. Lawrence, among others.

David Nokes (1948–2009) was a literary scholar who wrote biographies of Jonathan Swift and Jane Austen, among others. He adapted for the screen classic novels such as Samuel Richardson's *Clarissa* and Anne Brontë's *The Tenant of Wildfell Hall* (1996).

Joyce Carol Oates's many books include *A Widow's Story: A memoir* (2011), and the novels *What I Lived For* (1994) and *Middle Age: A romance* (2001).

Peter Parker's books include *Ackerley* (1989) and *Housman Country: Into the heart of England* (2016).

Gwendoline Riley's novels include *Sick Notes* (2004), *Opposed*

Positions (2012) and *First Love* (2017).

Pat Rogers, Professor of English at the University of South Florida, edited *Pride and Prejudice* in the *Cambridge Edition of the Works of Jane Austen* (2006).

Peter Sabor, Professor of English at McGill University, edited *The Cambridge Companion to Emma* (2015).

Ian Sansom is a novelist, whose books include the Country Guides series of crime novels, and an Associate Professor at Trinity College Dublin.

Brian Southam (1931–2010) was a publisher and eminent Jane Austen scholar. His seminal study *Jane Austen's Literary Manuscripts* appeared in 1964.

A. E. Stallings is a poet living in Athens.

Kathryn Sutherland is Professor of Bibliography and Textual Criticism at St Anne's College, Oxford. Her publications include the edited collection *Jane Austen: Writer in the world* (2017).

Bharat Tandon served as a judge for the Man Booker Prize for Fiction in 2012. He is the author of *Jane Austen and the Morality of Conversation* (2003).

Stella Tillyard is a historian whose books include *Aristocrats* (1994) and *A Royal Affair: George III and his troublesome siblings* (2006).

Claire Tomalin is the author of several notable literary biographies; her subjects have included Samuel Pepys, Jane Austen, Charles Dickens and Katherine Mansfield.

Virginia Woolf (1882–1941) was a frequent contributor to the *TLS*. Her novels include *Mrs Dalloway* (1925) and *To the Lighthouse* (1927).

Northanger Abbey

volume 1, chapter 5

"And what are you reading, Miss – ?" "Oh! it is only a novel!" replies the young lady; while she lays down her book with affected indifference, or momentary shame. – "It is only Cecilia, or Camilla, or Belinda"; or, in short, only some work in which the greatest powers of the mind are displayed, in which the most thorough knowledge of human nature, the happiest delineation of its varieties, the liveliest effusions of wit and humour are conveyed to the world in the best chosen language.

Finished by 1803, Northanger Abbey wasn't published until 1817, after Jane Austen's death. It is celebrated for its parodying of Gothic novels, to which its heroine Catherine Morland is thoroughly addicted, although it also makes this spirited defence of novels – and perhaps suggests that there are life lessons to be learnt from fiction, after all.

ILLUSTRATION: **DARREN SMITH**

INTRODUCTORY ESSAY

A Jane of one's own

The *TLS* of May 8 1913 opened with the essay below, prompted by *Life and Letters of Jane Austen*, by W. and R. A. Austen-Leigh, and *Old Friend and New Fancies*, by Sybil G. Brinton. The anonymous author, Virginia Woolf, would go on to become one of Austen's great successors in the art of novel-writing

AUTHOR: **VIRGINIA WOOLF**

In many ways Jane Austen must be considered singularly blessed. The manner in which from generation to generation her descendants respect her memory is, we imagine, precisely that which she would have chosen for herself – and she would have been hard to please. In 1870 the Memoir by her nephew gave us not only the facts of her life, but reproduced the atmosphere in which that life was lived so instinctively that his book can never be superseded; and now once more the son and grandson of that nephew show themselves possessed to the full of the family taste and modesty. In this final biography, for surely no other will be possible, they have brought together all that is known about Jane Austen, basing their narrative, of course, upon the original memoir but completing it with the letters which appeared in Lord Brabourne's two volumes, and adding certain other letters, traditions and family histories. By doing so they have given depth and perspective to the figure which we see in our mind's eye; to say that they have told us anything fresh about her would not be true. Miss Cassandra Austen put that effectively

beyond their power. To her alone did Jane Austen write freely and impulsively; to her she must have expressed the hopes and, if the rumour is true, the one keen disappointment of her life; but when Miss Cassandra Austen grow old and suspected that a time might come when strangers would be curious about her sister's private affairs, she burnt, at great cost to herself, every letter which could gratify their curiosity. The letters which remain exist simply because she thought that no one; not even the nephews and nieces, would be sufficiently interested in Jane Austen to disturb them. Had she guessed that they would not only be read but published, that many thousands would enjoy the wit and ransack every sentence for revelations, we may be sure that she would have flung them also on to the flames with one sweep of her arm.

This being so, we are aware that it is a confession which is made when we say that we are sufficiently interested in Jane Austen to wish to know everything that it is possible to know about her. We are grateful to little Philadelphia Austen, who describes Jane as "not at all pretty

RIGHT
Virginia Woolf, 1920s

and very prim, unlike a girl of twelve .... Jane is whimsical and affected"; and to old Mrs Mitford, who remembered the Austens as girls and knew Jane as "the prettiest, silliest, most affected, husband-hunting butterfly she ever remembers", and to Miss Mitford's properly anonymous friend

who visits her now [and] says that she has stiffened into the most perpendicular, precise, taciturn piece of "single blessedness" that ever existed, and that, until *Pride and Prejudice* showed what a precious gem was hidden in that unbending case, she was no more regarded in society than a poker or a firescreen .... The case is very different now; she is still a poker – but a poker of whom everybody is afraid .... A wit [the good lady exclaims, and we cannot help hoping with more reason than she knew of at the time], a delineator of character, who does not talk, is terrific indeed!

Of course, these critics are wrong, but it is amusing to see as clearly as we do why they went wrong. Finally we are ready to bless Marianne Knight perpetually for having recalled not very many years ago how "Aunt Jane would

GETTY

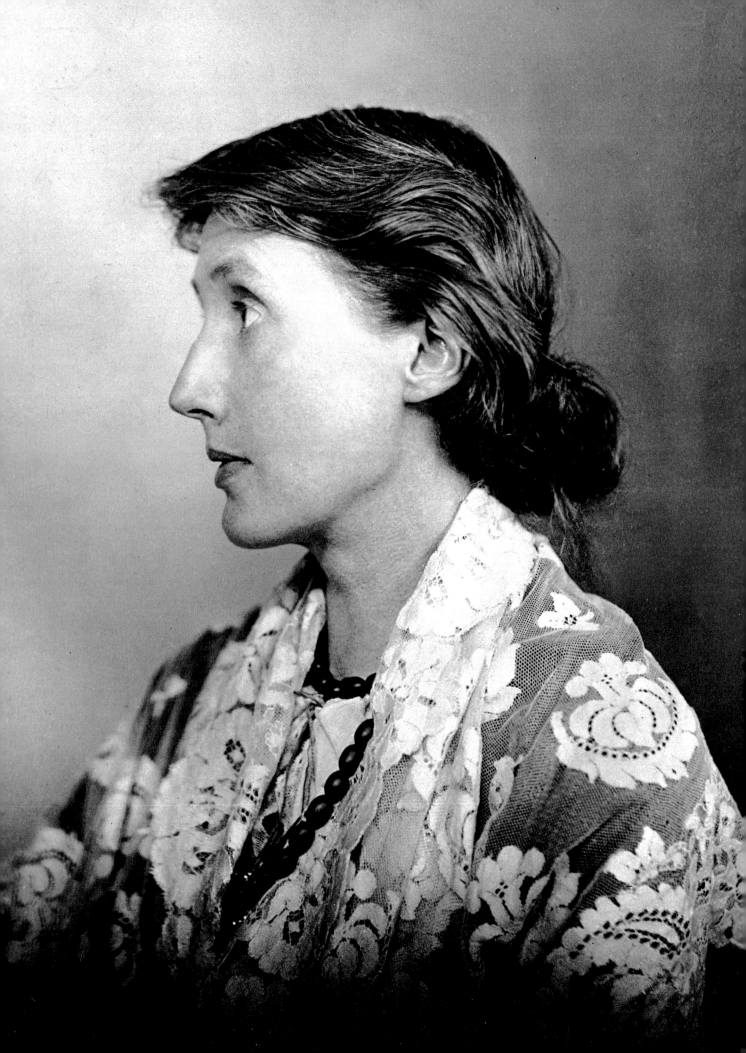

sit very quietly at work beside the fire in the Godmersham library, then suddenly burst out laughing, jump up, cross the room to a distant table with papers lying on it, write something down, returning presently and sitting down quietly to her work again". Was it then that Mrs Norris gave William "something considerable", or Lady Bertram had the happy idea of sending Chapman to help Miss Fanny? We are grateful for trifles, in short, for it is by means of such trifles that we draw a little closer to the charm, the brilliance, the strength and sincerity of character that lay behind the novels. For the rest, we cannot grudge Jane and Cassandra the glance of satisfaction which they must cast at each other as after fresh scrutiny of that serene and smiling face we turn away baffled, and they know that their secrets are their own for ever. We need not be surprised that even the jealous Cassandra had no inkling of the

curiosity of the generations to come. So lately as 1870 there was only one complete edition of the novels, and the taste for them was a gift that ran in families and was a mark of rather peculiar culture. Today things have changed so far that the present biography is the third work about Jane Austen that has been published in the course of the year. One, by Miss Brinton. takes the original form of continuing the fortunes of the characters and devising marriages between them – a work of great love and great ingenuity which, if taken not as fiction but as talk about Jane Austen's characters, will please that select public which is never tired of discussing them.

But the time has come, surely, when there is no need to bring witnesses to prove Jane Austen's fame. Arrange the great English novelists as one will, it does not seem possible to bring them out in any order where she is not first,

ABOVE
Tom and Jerry
"sporting a toe" at a
London ball (1823)
by Robert and
George Cruikshank

or second, or third, whoever her companions may be. Unlike other great writers in almost every way, she is unlike them, too, in the very slow and very steady rise of her reputation; it has been steady because there is probably no novelist of the nineteenth century who requires us to make so little excuse for her, and it has been slow because she has limitations of a kind particularly likely to cramp a writer's popularity. The mere sight of her six neat volumes suggests something of the reason, for when we look at them we do not remember any page or passage which so burnt itself into our minds when we read it first that from time to time we take the book down, read that sentence again, and are again exalted. We doubt whether one of her novels was over a long toil and stumble to any reader with a splendid view at the end. She was never a revolution to the young, a stern comrade, a brilliant and extravagantly

admired friend, a writer whose sentences sang in one's brain and were half absorbed into one's blood. And directly one has set down any of the above phrases one is conscious of the irony with which she would have disclaimed any such wish or intention. We can hear it in the words addressed to the nephew who had lost two chapters of his novel. "How could I possibly join them on to the little bit (two inches wide) of ivory on which I

> **"**
> *When she is pointing out where her people are bad, weak, faulty . . . she is winged and inapproachable*
>
> VIRGINIA WOOLF

work with so fine a brush, as produces little effect after much labour?"; and again in the famous, "Let other pens dwell on guilt and misery. I quit such odious subjects as soon as I can".

But however modest and conscious of her own defects she may be, the defects are there and must be recognized by readers who are as candid as Jane Austen herself would wish them to be. The chief reason why she does not appeal to us as some inferior writers do is that she has too little of the rebel in her composition, too little discontent, and of the vision which is the cause and the reward of discontent. She seems at times to have accepted life too calmly as she found it, and to any one who reads her biography or letters it is plain that life showed her a great deal that was smug, commonplace, and, in a bad sense of the word, artificial. It showed her a world made up of big houses and little houses, of gentry inhabiting them who were keenly

conscious of their grades of gentility, while life itself consisted of an interchange of tea parties, picnics and dances, which eventually, if the connexion was respectable and the income on each side satisfactory, led to a thoroughly suitable marriage. It happens very seldom, but still it does happen, that we feel that the play of her spirit has been hampered by such obstacles; that she believes in them as well as laughs at them, and that she is debarred from the most profound insight into human nature by the respect which she pays to some unnatural convention. There are characters such as the characters of Elinor Dashwood and Fanny Price which bore us frankly; there are pages which, though written in excellent English, have to be skipped; and those defects are due to the fact that she is content to take it for granted that such characters and conduct are good without trying to see them in a fresh light for herself.

But the chief damage which this conservative spirit has inflicted on her art is that it tied her hands together when she dealt with men. Her heroes were less the equals of her heroines than should have been the case, making allowance for the fact that so it must always be when a woman writes of men or a man of women. It is where the power of the man has to be conveyed that her novels are always at their weakest; and the heroines themselves lose something of their life because in moments of crisis they have for partners men who are inferior to them in vitality and character. A clergyman's daughter in those days was, no doubt, very carefully brought up, and in no other age, we imagine, were men and woman less at their ease together; still, it rests with the novelists to break down the barriers; it is they who should imagine what they cannot know even at the risk of making themselves superbly ridiculous. Miss Austen, however, was so fastidious, so conscious of her own limitations, that when she found out that hedges do not grow in Northamptonshire she eliminated her hedge rather than run the risk of inventing one which could not exist. This is the more annoying because we are inclined to think that she could have run almost all the risks and triumphed. In proof of this we might quote two passages from *Mansfield Park* (the first is quoted by Professor Bradley in his lecture to the English Association), where, forsaking her usual method, she suddenly hazards herself in a strange new atmosphere and breathes into her work a spirit of beauty and romance. Fanny Price standing at a window with Edmund breaks into a strange rhapsody, which begins, "Here's harmony! here's repose! here's what may leave all painting and all music behind, and what poetry only can attempt to describe!" &c. And, again, she throws a curious

atmosphere of symbolism over the whole scene where Maria and Henry Crawford refuse to wait for Rushworth, who is bringing the key of the gate. "But unluckily", Maria exclaims, "that iron gate, that ha-ha gives me a feeling of restraint and hardship, I cannot get out, as the starling said."

But those limitations are noticeable only when Jane Austen is committing herself to saying seriously that such things and such people are good, which in the works of any writer is a dangerous moment, leading us to hold our breath; when she is pointing out where they are bad, weak, faulty, exquisitely absurd she is winged and inapproachable. Her heroes may be insipid, but think of her fools! Think of Mr Collins, Mr Woodhouse, Miss Bates, Mrs Norris, Mrs Bennet, and in a lesser degree of Mrs Allen, Lady Bertram, Sir William Lucas! What a light the thought of them will cast on the wettest day! How various and individual is their folly! For they are no more consistently foolish than people in real life. It is only that they have a peculiar point of view, and that when health, or economy, or ladies of title are mentioned, as must frequently happen in the world we live in, they give vent to their views to our eternal delight; but there are a great many circumstances in which they do not behave foolishly at all. Indeed, we are inclined to think that the most painful incident in any of the novels is when Miss Bates's feelings are

66

People could never be too absurd, life never too full of humours and singularities for her taste

VIRGINIA WOOLF

PETER SMITH, JANE AUSTEN HOUSE MUSEUM, ALAMY

BELOW
The table, in the dining room at Chawton, where Jane Austen wrote and revised her novels

hurt at the picnic, and, turning to Mr Knightley, she says, "I must have made myself very disagreeable or she would not have said such a thing to an old friend". Again, when they are discussing the study of human nature and Darcy remarks, "But people themselves alter so much that there is something to be observed in them for ever", Mrs Bennet's reply is surely a stroke of genius. "'Yes, indeed', cried Mrs Bennet, offended by his manner of mentioning a country neighbourhood, 'I assure you there is quite as much of *that* going on in the country as in town.'" Such is the light it throws upon the muddled vacuity of the poor lady's mind that she ceases to be ridiculous and becomes almost tragic in her folly.

It came so naturally to Jane Austen to describe people by means of their faults that had there been a drop of bitterness in her spirit her novels would have given us the most consistently satirical picture of life that exists. Open them where you will, you are almost certain to light upon some passage exquisitely satirising the absurdities of life – satirizing them, but without bitterness, partly no doubt because she was happy in her life, partly because she had no wish that things should be other than they are. People could never be too absurd, life never too full of humours and singularities for her taste, and as for telling people how they ought to live, which is the satiric motive, she would have held up her hands in amazement at the thought. Life itself – that was the object of her love, of her absorbed study; that was the pursuit which filled those unrecorded years and drew out the "quiet intensity of her nature", making her appear to the outer world a little critical and aloof, and "at times very grave". More than any other novelist she fills every inch of her canvas with observation, fashions every sentence into meaning, stuffs up every

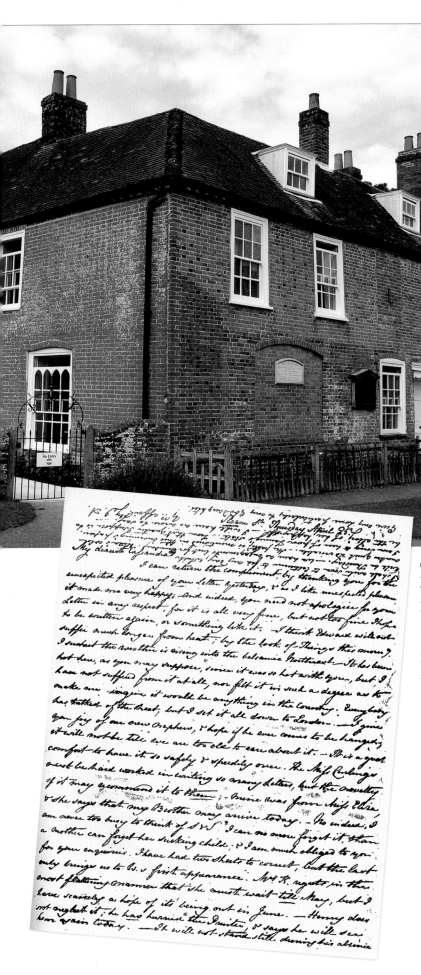

ABOVE
Chawton Cottage;
Austen moved
there in 1809

LEFT
A letter from Austen
to Cassandra,
April 25 1811

chink and cranny of the fabric until each novel is a little living world, from which you cannot break off a scene or even a sentence without bleeding it of some of its life. Her characters are so rounded and substantial that they have the power to move out of the scenes in which she placed them into other moods and circumstances. Thus, if some one begins to talk about Emma Woodhouse or Elizabeth Bennet voices from different parts of the room begin, saying which they prefer and why, and how they differ, and how they might have acted if one had been at Box Hill and the other at Rosings, and where they live, and how their houses are disposed, as if they were living people. It is a world, in short, with houses, roads, carriages, hedgerows, copses, and with human beings.

All this was done by a quiet maiden lady who had merely paper and ink at her disposal; all this is conveyed by little sentences between inverted commas and smooth paragraphs of print. Only those who have realized for themselves the ridiculous inadequacy of a straight stick dipped in ink when brought in contact with the rich and tumultuous glow of life can appreciate to the full the wonder of her achievement, the imagination, the penetration, the insight, the courage, the sincerity which are required to bring before us one of those perfectly normal and simple incidents of average human life. Besides all these gifts and more wonderful than any of them, for without it they are apt to run to waste, she possessed in a greater degree perhaps than any other English woman the sense of the significance of life apart from any personal liking or disliking; of the beauty and continuity which underlies its trivial stream. A little aloof, a little inscrutable and mysterious, she will always remain, but serene and beautiful also because of her greatness as an artist. ▪

A life at a glance

Jane Austen's life and works, from cradle to grave (via teenage satire, a rejected proposal and publishing success)

ILLUSTRATION: **MARTIN HAAKE**

1775
Jane Austen born on December 16 in the village of Steventon in Hampshire, the seventh of eight children.

1785
Austen and her elder sister Cassandra attend the Abbey House School in Reading, but are removed the following year.

1786
Austen begins writing stories, skits and verses in what will turn into a remarkable three-volume collection of early work.

1795
Austen starts to write a sequence of novels such as "Elinor and Marianne" – the basis of *Sense and Sensibility*.

1801
The Revd Austen, now retired, moves the family to Bath – to Jane's horror. (When told about it, she apparently fainted in shock.)

1802
Austen accepts a proposal of marriage from the Revd Harris Bigg-Wither, only to change her mind and refuse him.

1803
"Susan" is bought by a publisher who fails to publish it. Austen visits Lyme Regis, the Dorset town featured in *Persuasion*.

1804
Around now Austen starts, but later abandons, a novel called "The Watsons", of which the manuscript survives.

1805
The Revd Austen dies and is buried in Bath. "His tenderness as a father, who can do justice to?", Jane wrote of him.

1809
Mrs Austen and her daughters settle in Chawton, a Hampshire village near the manor house of Jane's brother Edward.

1811
Sense and Sensibility is published. Austen revises "First Impressions" as *Pride and Prejudice*.

1813
Pride and Prejudice is published, and receives some good "word of mouth" recommendations as well as the customary notices.

1814
Mansfield Park is published and sells out in six months (a second edition in 1816 also sells out). Austen begins writing *Emma*.

1815
Emma is published at the end of the year (with 1816 on the title page). It bears, by invitation, a dedication to the Prince Regent.

1816
Austen finishes *Persuasion* in the summer. Her famed contemporary Walter Scott enthusiastically reviews *Emma*.

1817
Austen dies on July 18, leaving her novel "Sanditon" unfinished. She is buried in Winchester Cathedral.

What does Jane Austen mean to you?

A selection of literary figures and *TLS* contributors tell us what they think of Jane Austen's work, both professionally and personally

Melvyn Bragg

I came late to Jane Austen. She was not on my O Level or A Level list in the 1950s, nor, as I remember, was she at all promoted by Mr Tillotson, the English Master (in every other respect a remarkable teacher). I read widely in the school and town libraries but – no Jane Austen. By the time I got to university my reading outside the curriculum was extensive but basically the Russian novelists, the American, French, Irish novelists, and as many comic novels as I could get my hands on, coupled with a conscientious desire to read English – the Brontës, Fielding, George Eliot, and Poets. Still no Jane Austen. The woman who became my first wife lodged with Professor Peter Strawson, and it was he who took me firmly by the hand and led me to the six books which a Philosopher colleague of his thought were the only works of English fiction worth reading.

I suppose I may have dodged or ducked Jane Austen for what now seem to be silly or spurious class reasons or a foolish and mistaken notion of what she might be like. Certainly if I had any thoughts back then up to the age of

twenty-one, it would be that – compared with D. H. Lawrence and Thomas Hardy and Thomas Mann . . .

But then I got hooked and have stayed hooked. Sometimes she is so good it's unbearable and I have to put the book down for a while. The older I got and the better reader I became, and the more I get from her. And she just gets better! Television adaptations have led her to mass audiences and she has thrived there as well. She is incomparable.

Geoff Dyer

We did *Emma* for A-Level so it was one of the first serious novels I ever read. In a sense, then, Jane Austen is literature to me. She was not just one of the first novelists I read but also the oldest, i.e. earliest. You can start further back, of course, but romping through *Tom Jones* feels like a bit of a waste of olde time in the way that *Persuasion* never does. I associate reading Austen with a consciousness of the gap between my limited life experience – swilling beer, basically – and the expanded grasp of the psychological subtleties and nuances of situations and relationships

that her books gradually revealed. But I'm conscious also of a different kind of gap: that between the riches afforded by the novels and the tedium of the criticism served up alongside them. Macmillan Casebooks – anthologies of critical essays – were the default educational tools even though most of the pieces in the one on *Emma* are complete dross. The process whereby "doing English" morphed into "doing criticism" began with Austen and continued all the way through university. Was this a purposeful deterrent? George Steiner is right: the best critical essay on Jane Austen is *Middlemarch*.

Whereas my head is full of Shakespeare, only a few lines from Austen have stayed with me – the very ones, predictably, that had us smirking at school: "Anne had always found such a style of intercourse highly imprudent" (*Persuasion*), or Mr Elton "making violent love" to Emma in a carriage.

Amit Chaudhuri

It's astonishing how much writers owe to Jane Austen. Most love her, and rush to claim her, and even the few who

ALAMY, GETTY, REX, SHUTTERSTOCK, PETER SMITH/JANE AUSTEN'S HOUSE MUSEUM

don't (principally because they're ignorant of her work) have to admit she's been important to them in some way. I belong to the second category. It was my search for an alternative to Austen that took me, eventually, to a way of writing about the world and place that I found in D. H. Lawrence's *Sons and Lovers*. My avoidance of Austen came not from an enlightened critique of her work, but strategic disengagement; this disengagement was as important to me as embracing *Sons and Lovers* would be later. Austen portrayed a kind of provincial English life which I neither had a place in nor recognized. Her drawing room and its conversations denoted an interiority in which I felt unwelcome: not just because I am Indian, but because of the peculiarities of my temperament. At the Morels', I felt at home – not because I'd grown up in such a home in Bombay, but because, in the way the smell of linen being ironed or the sound of Walter Morel's whistling drifted from room to room, I was reminded, subconsciously, of my uncle's house in Calcutta. Provincial modernity brought me joy: it was one of the things

Lawrence helped me understand. Austen helped me, too, because her notion of the province was so powerfully different.

Tessa Hadley

Jane Austen's innovations in the novel-form in English are as significant and form-changing as, let's say, as Beethoven's in music. He imagined a whole new sound world; Austen imagines a new world of fluid novelistic mimesis, brings it into being and makes it in the same moment seem inevitable and natural as breathing. Flaubert is often credited with inventing "indirect free style", where the language from sentence to sentence flows almost imperceptibly out of the author's words and thoughts into the character's, and back again – but Austen does it in the English novel decades earlier. Just to take one example: in *Mansfield Park*, when Fanny is watching the man she loves falling for Mary Crawford, we can observe from a wry distance the poignant comedy of Fanny's feelings and actually inhabit them at the same time, experience her feelings from the inside. "Edmund was close to [Mary]; he

was speaking to her; he was evidently directing her management of the bridle; he had hold of her hand; [Fanny] saw it, or the imagination supplied what the eye could not reach." The English novel has been wonderful before Austen, but the narrator has always been mediator and interpreter, getting in the way of the life observed, intruding upon it. Suddenly under Austen's treatment the scene is filmic, immersive, giving an illusion of unfolding in an immediate present (though of course not in the present tense, which isn't needed). The illusion is so powerful that it seems as if anything could happen next – even if we remember how it all must end. This radical openness lifts the novel form to a new level of possibility.

Joyce Carol Oates

Brilliantly witty, a master (mistress?) of the deftly turned sentence, Jane Austen is the very spirit of "civilized" English society. She invites us to laugh – though not cruelly – at human foibles. She holds up a mirror that flatters even as it chides. Very kindly she allows us to imagine ourselves "superior" – for she has invited us to be her confidante; we are safely on her side. Her satire is a light whip that will never draw blood. The very tone of Austen's prose assures us that we will not be shocked with scenes of anguish or despair within her pages, still less with bloodstained sheets following horrific stillbirths, or violent rapes; no one will be slapped, kicked, bullied, crushed; we will never witness acts of murder, nor even hear of such acts, though (we can assume) many murders were being committed beyond the radar of the Austen novels in the service of the British empire at the time of their composition. We love Austen as the white "feminine" fantasy that stirs even (some) feminists to nostalgia for a world of good daughters, good wives, good mothers, and good, poised prose that never falters, stumbles, decays, effloresces, or soars.

Peter Parker

"Oh! It is only a novel!" a young lady replies when asked in *Northanger Abbey* what she is reading. Jane Austen's spirited rejoinder is one of the most perfect defences of fiction by one of its very best practitioners: "in short, only some work in which the greatest powers of the mind are displayed, in which the most thorough knowledge of human nature, the happiest delineation of its varieties, the liveliest effusions of wit and humour, are conveyed to the world in the best-chosen language". I can think of no better account of what one wants from a novel, and of what Austen repeatedly provides in hers. Her witty and subversive delineation of male complacency and self-satisfaction is exhilarating, and she proves by example that, contrary to what many men continue to believe, the domestic arena is entirely suited to serious fiction. By taking "three or four families in a country village", and closely observing their relations to each other, suitors, money and social position, she provides

an analysis of the world more penetrating, and often more truly shocking, than many so-called novels of ideas. If in their conclusions the novels conform to Miss Prism's definition of fiction, the means by which these are reached are complex, unexpected and completely satisfying.

Gwendoline Riley

I reach for *Persuasion* when I'm confined, by illness or bad weather. The novel begins by informing us that Sir Walter Elliot "never took up any book but the Baronetage". He likes to re-read his own entry and anticipate its prolongation; he also looks at those lines which have not lasted, an activity which sees "any unwelcome sensations . . . changed naturally into pity and contempt". As a reader – and re-reader – of *Persuasion*, my motives are not so mean though perhaps just as utilitarian. The results are so reliable. I'm pierced by Anne Elliot's isolation. That family! Her forlorn, unanswered question, finding herself a spare wheel on a group outing: "Is not this one of the ways to Winthrop?" I'm on to the meaning of Captain Wentworth's off-handedness and wince at "shy" Captain Benwick, the poetry buff whose interest Anne rouses by being polite and solicitous: he moves as if on castors, once he has his object . . . . Jane Austen was too generous to trifle with us. Her characters know the price of everything, and the shrewd or sensible ones discern value, too, but they are not in the majority. Therein lies the comedy: sly, savage, or festive, and the poignancy and pain in these books.

A. E. Stallings

To reread Jane Austen is to remember what it is like to be young. I can think of no writer who better understands teenagers and young people, especially young women, their earnestness and

cattiness, extremes of joy and heartbreak, their boredom and intrigues. I get older, but the novels keep their dewy bloom. Of late I have been thinking of Catherine in *Northanger Abbey*. She lacks Lizzy's sprezzatura, the Eliot pride, an abundance of sense or sensibility, is not headstrong like Emma, nor as upright as Fanny. Catherine is an anti-heroine, an every-girl. A tomboy at fourteen, she loves "cricket, baseball, riding on horseback, and running about the country", and reading, as long the books are all narrative and no information. At seventeen, prettier and better washed, she still devours gothic romances. Austen is affectionate rather than condescending towards this "chick lit", even as it gets Catherine into trouble. Today, Catherine would no doubt be engrossed in the *Twilight* series or its imitators, all vampires, werewolves, and love story. I picture her modern counterpart (my daughter in a few years) reading in a window-seat, suspended in the present and eager to find out what happens next.

Adam Thirlwell

I think she is one of the greatest novelists and I have no idea how to talk about her. I love the way Virginia Woolf once wrote – of her juvenilia! – "Whatever she writes is finished and turned and set in its relation, not to the parsonage, but to the universe. She is

It's astonishing how much writers owe to Jane Austen. Most love her, and rush to claim her

AMIT CHAUDHURI

impersonal; she is inscrutable". The best way of talking about Jane Austen would find a way of folding two observations inside each other: a literary observation of her – but what exactly? – linguistic precision, refusal of stylistic afflatus; and an economic observation of her power analysis, the way money is distributed inside her couples as silently as sex. But I don't know if we have a vocabulary adequate to the kind of severity she invented. She makes you realize how romantic pretension and economic pretension are dirtily related, or even versions of the same thing. Maybe what this means is that she needs a literary criticism that is really anthropology: these novels, so elegant, so artificial, so finished, are also live contemporary toys – like fetishes, or like those alien transmitters still emitting information in our futuristic horror movies. And one proof of this is that the greatest modern version of her fiction is still the indie trash of *Clueless*: where the backdrop to the universal isn't the parsonage but the malls of Beverly Hills.

Pat Rogers
On the rebound from a teenage crush – fixated with French literature of the nineteenth century – I came back to Austen for A levels and fell for *Emma*. The novel showed me, contrary to a big lie of some versions of modernism I'd imbibed, that you can have cultivated form, propriety of manner, symmetry in narrative and stylistic polish; yet still tell the truth about messy human lives. Austen taught me one big thing, along with Mozart, Shakespeare, and Rodgers & Hart sung by Ella Fitzgerald. Conventions are not just things to break, subvert, hide, or burlesque. Rather, high art can enlist and inhabit convention to its own purposes. How this works in actual practice emerged most clearly later from Charles Rosen's book on *The Classical Style*. But it was with Austen

that the breakthrough came, as I belatedly grasped that making it new doesn't have to mean a complete artistic retooling. Mr Weston's good wine never tasted more fresh on the palate than served in an old vessel.

Peter Sabor
In March 1817, just four months before her death, Jane Austen wrote to her favourite niece, Fanny Knight, telling her that "pictures of perfection make me sick and wicked". She would surely have been sickened by her brother Henry's patently false claim, published in a memoir prefixed to the posthumous 1818 edition of *Northanger Abbey* and *Persuasion*, that "every thing came finished from her pen". She failed to complete two of her novels, "The Watsons" and "Sanditon", and their surviving rough drafts show how heavily she revised and re-revised her work. She had a horror of mere replication. After telling her sister Cassandra, in a letter of February 1813, that the newly published *Pride and Prejudice* was "rather too light, and bright, and sparkling", she set to work on *Mansfield Park*, the darkest and least effervescent of her novels. Like Samuel Johnson, an important influence on her limpid prose, she was averse to cant in all its forms: the characters that come off worst in her novels are those who mouth words without thinking about their import. With her lifelong desire to create, to vary, and to improve upon herself, Austen represents, for me, all that a novelist and a human being should be.

Samantha Ellis
I was about twelve when I first encountered Lizzy Bennet. Growing up in a tight-knit, traditional community of Iraqi Jewish refugees, I understood the pressure to marry, and the terror that it would be impossible to square my parents' expectations with my own

romantic dreams. Lizzy gave me hope. I wanted to be her, all muddy petticoats and defiance. (I also wanted Mr Darcy, which proved unwise; it turns out that not all arrogant men are secretly lovely; some are just arrogant.) Lizzy's wit seemed a survival strategy I could usefully learn. Now I can see how cleverly Jane Austen warned that laughing too much could turn you into mindless Kitty or snarky Mr Bennet, who both fail to really take responsibility for their families. The backstory to *Pride and Prejudice* thrills me still; the first draft written at twenty, when Austen was in love with dashing lawyer Tom Lefroy, the second draft written at thirty-seven, when she had lost Lefroy for exactly the reasons Jane nearly loses Bingley, but had also found the courage to refuse to marry the wrong men. Austen also gave me the idea (via *Northanger Abbey*'s Catherine) that I didn't have to brave or brilliant just yet but could instead be "in training for a heroine", and that this might be a worthwhile lifelong quest.

Jocelyn Harris
Even after all these years, Jane Austen remains inexhaustible. Teaching cannot wither her, nor research stale her infinite variety. I especially admire her Shakespearean trick of breaking tension by comedy, as in *Persuasion*, where Anne Elliot feels someone lifting the child off her back – someone! – and Charles Hayter, grumpy that Captain Wentworth has succeeded where he could not, bumbles into her confusion and agitation. I share Anne's anxiety about the captain; I experience the overwhelming sensation of pleasure and pain that Austen calls "exquisite". Like Hermione in *The Winter's Tale*, Anne comes back to life. But eight-and-a-half years of happiness have been lost, as Wentworth spells out so precisely in his proposal. ∎

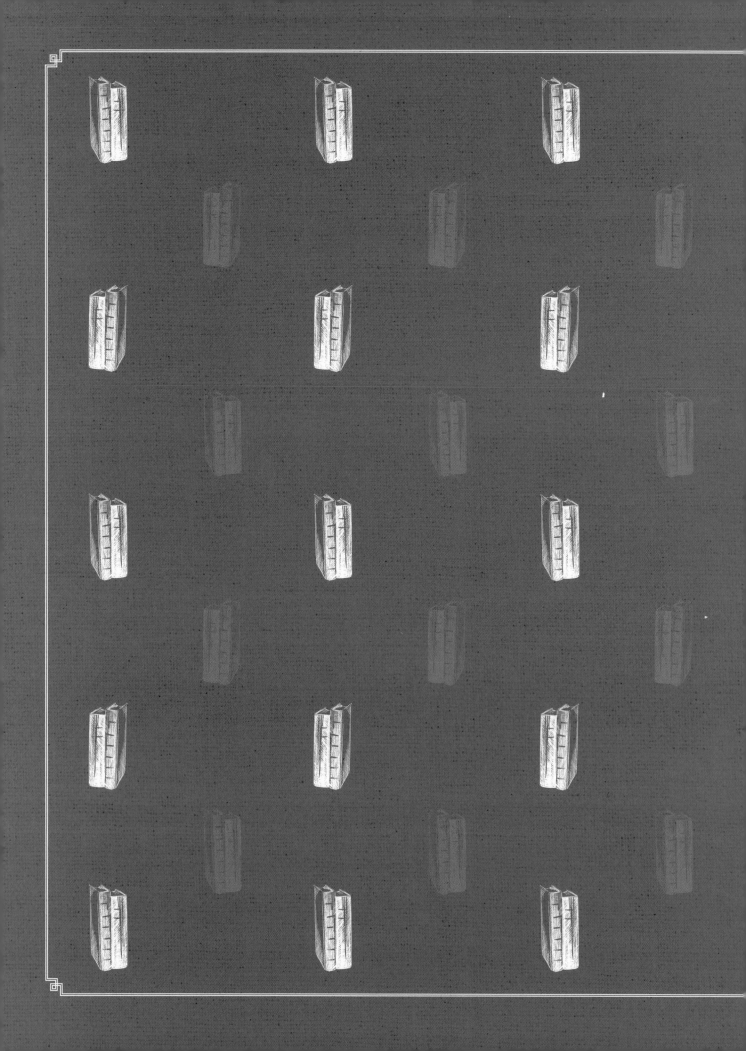

The Novels

THE NOVELS

We're all Janeites now

A novelist of the twenty-first century takes a fresh look
at Jane Austen's six major novels

AUTHOR: **IAN SANSOM**

"Anyone", wrote Virginia Woolf in *A Room of One's Own*, though of course she didn't mean "anyone" but "me", "who has the temerity to write about Jane Austen is aware of [two] facts: first, that of all great writers she is the most difficult to catch in the act of greatness; second, that there are twenty-five elderly gentlemen living in the neighbourhood of London who resent any slight upon her genius as if it were an insult to the chastity of their aunts."

Times have certainly changed: chaste aunts these days are about as rare as a "Bob's your uncle" and the twenty-five elderly gentlemen living in the neighbourhood of London who might resent you are now millions worldwide who are happy to abuse you on Twitter. We're all Janeites now: and if you're not, look out. In a world – to use a phrase that might serve as the introductory voice-over to the trailer for any recent Austen adaptation/biopic/retelling – in which the mute are always inglorious and fame is the only guarantee of value or quality, posterity has proved her worth. (Auden was right, as he was about most things, in "Letter to Lord Byron": "She wrote them for posterity, she said; / 'Twas rash, but by posterity she's read".) Which is why, like many writers before and since – obsessed with the mechanics and economics of reputation formation – Woolf was fascinated as much by Austen's fame as by her work. In a review in 1922 of a collection of Austen's early writing, *Love and Freindship*, Woolf opined that

All over England for the past ten or twenty years the reputation of Jane Austen has been accumulating on top of us like . . . quilts and blankets. The voices of the elderly and distinguished, of the clergy and the squierarchy, have droned in unison praising and petting, capping quotations, telling little anecdotes, raking up little facts. . . . So they pile up the quilts and counterpanes until the comfort becomes oppressive. Something must be done about it.

The metaphorical quilts and blankets of the squierarchy and the clergy have now become the films, the television series, the fine uniform and collector's editions, the appalling paperback editions, the fan fiction, the mugs, the ornaments, and indeed the actual quilts,

RIGHT
Illustrations by
H.M.Brock and
C.E.Brock to
*Sense and
Sensibility, Pride and
Predujice, Mansfield
Park, Emma,
Northanger Abbey*
and *Persuasion*

blankets, fleeces, snugglies, slippers, dressing gowns and pillow cases that are all part of the academic-entertainment complex devoted to the perpetuation of the memory of our dear Jane (or in Henry James's formulation, "their 'dear', our dear, everybody's, dear Jane"). There are in fact now so many books on the Austen phenomenon that they are themselves a phenomenon – from Eckart Voigts-Virchow's perfectly serious *Janespotting and Beyond: British heritage retrovisions since the mid-1990s* (2004) and Beatrice Battaglia and Diego Saglia's *Re-Drawing Austen: Picturesque travels in Austenland* (2004), to the truly epiphenomenal *Among the Janeites: A journey through the world of Jane Austen fandom* (2013) by Deborah Yaffe, and Maggie Lane's pitch-perfect *Growing Older with Jane Austen* (2014), a book with a title so brilliantly targeted at its intended audience that one might amend Alan Coren's old joke about the only books guaranteed to sell being about golf, cats and Nazis, to golf, cats, Nazis and Jane Austen.

"It is possible to say of Jane Austen", according to Lionel Trilling, writing

"The enjoyment of Elinor's company"
Chapter XLIX

"And this offer of marriage you have refused?"
Chap. XX

"Miss Price all alone!"
Chap. X.

> **❝** *Three or four families in a country village is the very thing to work on . . .*

"I was mad enough, however, to resent"
Chapter L

"Henry drove so well"
Chap XX

"With eyes of glowing entreaty fixed on her"
Chapter XXIII

back in the 1950s, "as perhaps one can say of no other writer, that the opinions which are held of her work are almost as interesting, and almost as important to think about, as the work itself." Almost. These days it might be possible for someone to spend their entire time studying and thinking about the many blogs and social media posts devoted to Austen without ever having to study or think about Austen herself – indeed, some PhD student at Poppleton is doubtless doing so even now. So, tweet me. "Jane Austen" has become a signifier of such high semiotic intensity, possessing such incredible power both within and outside the academy that it has finally become the ultimate fiction: money. As if she weren't already ubiquitous enough, you can now find Jane lurking in your pocket, on the £10 note, and also on commemorative £2 coins. When the new style £5 note was recently released, a small number of the notes were engraved with a special Austen micro-portrait, making each fiver, according to the *Daily Mail*, and my mother, worth approximately £50,000. Thus, men and women up and down the land were finally reduced to searching for Jane Austen with a magnifying glass.

Something really must be done about it. The first thing to do, as I have, is to return to the novels, in the hope that they might flush entirely from one's mind the horrid vision of an endless all-star omnibus Austen, in which Hugh Grant, Colin Firth, Michael Gambon, Anne Hathaway, Emma Thompson and Alison Steadman are for ever jumping in and out of chaises and dancing cotillions.

Like most other sane people, I own copies of the works of Austen that last got an outing in the frantic few weeks before having to sit an exam and regurgitate gobbets sprackled with undigested bits of Tony Tanner, Lord

David Cecil and Elaine Showalter's *A Literature of Their Own.* Since then, I seem to have acquired two extra copies of *Emma*, my *Mansfield Park* has gone missing, and the tangerine spine of my copy of the Penguin *Lady Susan/The Watsons/Sanditon* – bought new for 50 pence, presumably as a distraction from the impending exams – remains as crisp and unbroken as an old Lucozade wrapper, destined now to remain a worthless mint condition heirloom and a reminder of the gassy, dimpled hopes and dreams of the late twentieth century. Plus I had never knowingly read *Northanger Abbey.*

So to begin with the entirely unknown: *Northanger Abbey* is the work of a young woman with an eye on the main chance. Barbara Benedict and Deirdre Le Faye note in their edition of

ALAMY, REX FEATURES

BELOW
Emma and Mr
Knightley, by
C. E. Brock, 1898

the novel in the Cambridge University Press nine-volume edition of the complete works, that "between 1784 and 1818 no fewer than thirty-two novels had been published containing 'Abbey' in the title, not to mention many others using such related nouns as 'Convent', 'Monastery' or 'Priory', 'Abbot', 'Friar' or 'Nun'": for *Northanger Abbey*, read *Girl on a/with a/ in a Gothic House.*

Written during 1789/9 but not published until after Austen's death in 1817 – and originally titled Susan by Austen, then changed to Catherine, and finally given its published title by Austen's brother Henry and sister Cassandra, the first keepers of the flame, who clearly understood the importance of a contemporary-sounding and eye-catching title – the

novel is a fair representation of what Austen could and couldn't do. If you really don't like *Northanger Abbey*, I can now safely attest, you are not much going to enjoy the others. There is a lot of shifting about from place to place, from ball to carriage to garden to the Pump Rooms, with characters endlessly obliging and disobliging one another with their company and opinions. A good test for incipient Janeiteism would be to measure a reader's tolerance for something like General Tilney's invitation to Catherine to visit Northanger Abbey, which doesn't in fact occur until about halfway through the book: "Can you in short be prevailed on to quit this scene of public triumph and oblige your friend Eleanor with your company in Gloucestershire? I am almost ashamed to make the request,

ABOVE
Anne Hathaway
as Jane Austen
in *Becoming
Jane*, 2007

though its presumption would certainly appear greater to every creature in Bath than yourself". If you like this sort of fine-milled quibbling, you are going to love all things Jane: it's not what she says, it's the way that she says it. (E. M. Forster, a self-proclaimed "Austenite", rightly pointed out that the true Austen fan, like the regular churchgoer, "scarcely notices what is being said", anyway.) There are perhaps no books in English that are easier or more tempting to skim read, and no books which when skimmed so entirely lose their flavour.

Northanger Abbey is thus either the epitome of dullness – a parody performed ironically, when everyone knows a parody should really be deadly serious – or a profound lesson in how to read and an exquisite challenge to try to understand what is to be taken seriously and what is not. The sharp tongue is firmly in cheek from the first sentence of the first paragraph on the first page:

No one who had ever seen Catherine Morland in her infancy would have supposed her born to be an heroine. . . . Her father was a clergyman, without being neglected or poor, and a very respectable man, though his name was Richard. . . . Her mother was a woman of useful plain sense. . . . She had three sons before Catherine was born; and, instead of dying in bringing the latter into the world, as anybody might expect, she still lived on. . . .

You can just imagine Lucy Worsley saying this – can't you? – straight to

Jane Austen has now become the ultimate fiction: money

IAN SANSOM

camera, in a bonnet. It's not so much a tone as a procedure – or a tone that becomes a procedure, as in any comic routine – and is presumably what perplexed Joseph Conrad, who famously wrote to H. G. Wells asking, "What is all this about Jane Austen? What is there in her? What is it all about?" What's it all about is entirely the wrong question. What's it all about is what it's avoiding.

Which brings us to *Sense and Sensibility*, the first of Austen's novels to appear in print, in 1811, and possessed of perhaps the longest, slowest swerve in all of her work, which is always happily detouring – taking three volumes and 300 careful pages to unsettle the Dashwoods ("The family of Dashwood had long been settled in Sussex", begins the book), only then to plant them safely elsewhere (sisters Elinor and Marianne end up happily married in Devonshire and Dorset). C. S. Lewis believed that one of Austen's great strengths – her moral virtue – was being able to write about the boring without being boring, though *Sense and Sensibility* tests this undoubtedly remarkable skill to the very limit. Plot summary, for the sake of those few remaining out there entirely unconvinced and un-Austened, would be both pointless and impossible, since the obvious and deliberate parallels and doublings and triplings of various excursions and encounters and indeed conversations is a structural principle which entirely determines the book's long drift through endless scenes designed to explore and explain the sense of "sense" and "sensibility".

"Seen in bare outline the plot displays a good deal of geometry", according to Tony Tanner, who even now – many years after his indispensable introductions to the old Penguin editions have been superseded by introductions by scholars more

Sense and Sensibility

Prde and Prejudice

Mansfield Park

up-to-date and au fait with all sorts of new-fangled theories and Austen fun facts – is never to be contradicted on the question of the novel, except perhaps to suggest that geometry is not necessarily something to be admired in a novel, and that, to borrow the language of the discussion of the picturesque between Elinor, Marianne and the dull and awkward Edward, an attention to geometry tends to produce a flatland populated by "tidy happy villagers" rather than wild prairies thronging with banditti.

Among the work of the great English novelists, Austen's are undoubtedly the books most easily reduced to geometric patterns and simple visual representation, which presumably explains their success on television and film, adapted by anyone and everyone with even the most primitive grasp of a story arc and Freytag's pyramid. (In Nabokov's lecture on *Mansfield Park*, published in *Lectures on Literature*, he usefully provides diagrams of the gardens and house at Sotherton, and his own teaching copy of the book – now in the Berg Collection at New York Public Library – is so densely annotated with maps and marks noting key points and turning places that it looks like a cross between some Syd Field scriptnotes on "beats" and a madman's illustrated guide to the world of Regency England.) Austen's genius, though, is that even the architecture of the books is ironic – "she is without exception vague, when it comes to describing buildings", complained Pevsner, though he admired her handling of perspective, derived from William Gilpin – and so one feels rather like a plodding Edward even to consider raising a complaint about her rather ludicrous structures. "Because he believes many people pretend to more admiration of the beauties of nature than they really feel, and is disgusted with such pretensions,

he affects greater indifference and less discrimination in viewing them himself than he possesses."

Pride and Prejudice (1813) is another of what I always thought of as the early novels – written by Austen during her twenties – though scholars such as Kathryn Sutherland have pointed out that because of the complex composition and publication history of the books, "there is no seamless division into early, middle and late writing, but instead a vital and unexpected revision of material over a considerable period" ("Chronology of Composition and Publication", in *Jane Austen in Context*, edited by Janet Todd). What doesn't seem to change over any period, either in Austen's writing, or indeed over the course of one's own sporadic return to the books – and what strikes one particularly forcefully in *Pride and Prejudice* – is the obsession with money.

Austen's writing, at the risk of stating the obvious, if not always about money, was always about money. "The first of all English games is making money", according to Ruskin, and Austen was nothing if not gamesome. (For a full – relentless – elaboration on Austen's brilliant strategic thinking, and a fine set of Austen-inspired decision tree diagrams to add to your own vast personal collection of Austen oddities, maps, charts and other curiosities and digi-hum delights, see Michael Chwe's *Jane Austen, Game Theorist*, 2013.) "You will be glad", she wrote to her brother Frank, after the publication of *Sense and Sensibility* in 1813, "that every Copy of S & S is sold & that it has brought me £140 – besides the Copyright, if that shd ever be of any value. – I have now therefore written myself into £250. – which only makes me long for more." The longing for more, of course, became a longing for more and more and more, so that by the time of the publication of *Pride and Prejudice* she was prepared to give up even her authorial anonymity for the promise of financial reward, as she explained again to Frank: "I shall not even attempt to tell Lies about it. – I shall rather try to make all the Money than all the Mystery I can of it – People shall pay for their Knowledge if I can make them".

And my, how we must pay: Austen's fans often remark that reading the novels feels like meeting with an old friend, but it also feels like meeting with a financial advisor, or your more successful sister-in-law. You are constantly bombarded with figures. Money in Austen is a language, it talks: it not only enables all the necessary connections and communications between characters, greasing the wheels of every curricle and barouche-landau, it enables all the ends eventually to meet; the books, after all, are about fortunes finding wives, and vice versa. If anything, the obsession with money – for those many of us like Miss Bates in *Emma*, who are worried about the costs of care for our dependents – makes Austen more, rather than less readable, since, as the Tory Party election manifesto has recently proved, only people who don't have to worry about money don't worry about money.

Mansfield Park (1814), next up after *Pride and Prejudice* – requiring a replacement purchase on my part, at the small price of a £10-note Jane for a Jane – I have to say, like almost everyone else, I found the most utterly unendearing of all of Austen's works.

Emma *represents the yin-yang of the Austen universe*

IAN SANSOM

Returning to Austen after half a lifetime, half-expecting the half-remembered bite of a Wilde, one is pleasantly surprised to be more often rewarded with the subtle taste of something more like Montaigne in novel form, but here all we get is dull old Fanny. Reading *Mansfield Park* immediately after having read *Pride and Prejudice*, one can't help but unfavourably compare the tale of self-flagellating Fanny Price with Austen's account of the thrill of the chase between Lizzy and Mr Darcy, and one also soon despairs of finding anything interesting or original to say about the book that hasn't been said better by many others, including, of course, Lionel Trilling, and Edward Said, and Marilyn Butler, and Nabokov: the book is not so much a novel as a testing ground for various critical positions and theories, including perhaps for Austen's own. I am assured by learned friends that my impatience with the book is a sign of my own immaturity and superfluity and that one day, if I'm lucky, I'll come to appreciate it, but in the meantime, and assuming the worst, let's move on directly to *Emma* (1815) which, thank goodness, is quite obviously a masterpiece and recognizably so even by thrill-seeking dullards with short attention spans.

Of all Austen's novels, *Emma* is perhaps the most entirely engaging, the book in which her dexterity of thought is at its most truly dextrous and her contradictory energies most thoroughly enlivening. Her strong satiric impulse to emphasize the chaos of life is perfectly balanced with her novelistic impulse to pattern, to scheme and to tidy. George Henry Lewes, writing in 1852 and naming her "the greatest artist that has ever written", understood Austen's limits – "she has risked no failures by attempting to delineate that which she has not seen" – but correctly

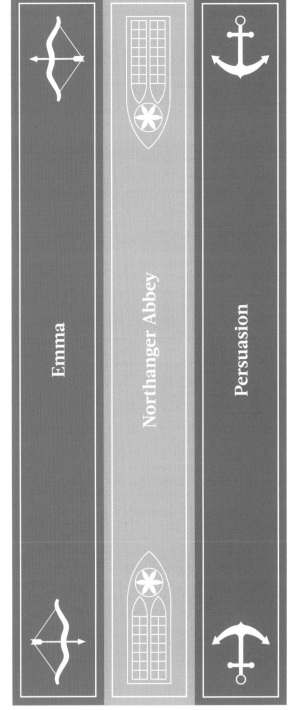

adjudged "Her world is a perfect orb, and vital", and no book of Austen's is more perfectly orb-like than *Emma*. It represents the yin-yang of the Austen universe.

With Emma busy projecting her fancies and fantasies onto others, even more disastrously than Catherine in *Northanger Abbey*, this is the novel in which Austen comes closest to a rounded presentation not only of human society but also of human consciousness. There are certainly no spasms of rapture and self-revelation of the kind one finds in, say, show-boating Charlotte Brontë, which is exactly why Brontë thought Austen "insensible" and "incomplete" (though surely G. K. Chesterton was correct, that Austen is, in fact, "stronger, sharper and shrewder"). "Anything like warmth or enthusiasm", Brontë complained,

anything energetic, poignant, heartfelt, is utterly out of place in commending these works: all such demonstrations the authoress would have met with a well-bred sneer, would have calmly scorned as outré or extravagant. . . . The passions are perfectly unknown to her: she rejects even a speaking acquaintance with that stormy sisterhood. . . What sees keenly, speaks aptly, moves flexibly, it suits her to study: but what throbs fast and full, though hidden, what the blood rushes through, what is the unseen seat of life and the sentient target of death – this Miss Austen ignores.

Wrong. Wrong. Wrong. And wrong again. There is very little throbbing or blood rushing in Austen, but this hardly means that the passions are unknown to her, as is best displayed in *Emma* in the famous passage in which the protagonist reflects on Mr Elton's marriage proposal:

The hair was curled, and the maid sent away, and Emma sat down to think and be

---

RIGHT
"Benwick sits at her elbow, reading verses . . ." (*Persuasion*) *Illustration by* Hugh Thomson, 1897.

BELOW
"What is there of good to be expected?" said he, taking the letter from his pocket; "but perhaps you would like to read it." (*Pride and Prejudice*)

---

miserable. – It was a wretched business indeed! – Such an overthrow of every thing she had been wishing for! – Such a development of every thing most unwelcome! – Such a blow for Harriet! – that was the worst of all. Every part of it brought pain and humiliation, of some sort or other; but, compared with the evil to Harriet, all was light; and she would gladly have submitted to feel yet more mistaken – more in error – more disgraced by mis-judgment, than she actually was, could the effects of her blunders have been confined to herself.

Emma here and elsewhere is most entirely herself, and the stormy sisterhood: "what she was, must be uncertain; but who she was, might be found out".

The representation of character in *Persuasion* (1817) seems at first to represent a step back towards Austen's youthful, lightly comic sketch mode, her silhouette method, with the description of Sir Walter Elliot, "a man who, for his own amusement, never took up any book but the Baronetage; there he found occupation for an idle hour, and consolation in a distressed one". But the satire soon becomes rather shaded and profound, so much so that *Persuasion*, in its tale of Anne Elliot, "a very pretty girl" with "every beauty excepting bloom", and her on-off relationship with Captain Wentworth, and the contrast between navy and gentry, and all the subtle shifts in hierarchy and power, becomes perhaps the most complex and bitter of the novels. It more than bears out Woolf's insight, in her essay "Personalities" (collected in *The Moment and Other Essays*, 1947), about Austen's "sense of meaning withheld, a smile at something unseen, an atmosphere of perfect control and courtesy mixed with something finely satirical, which, were it not directed against things in general, rather than

---

against individuals would be almost malicious, would, so I feel, make it alarming to find her at home".

In *Persuasion* we find Austen most uneasily at home (the book is largely set in Bath, a place of "imprisonment" for Anne and which Austen herself described in a letter to her sister Cassandra as a scene of "vapour, shadow, smoke and confusion"), though it should probably be added that when it comes to writers you wouldn't want to find at home, Woolf is certainly up there with Austen. Ivy Compton-Burnett, no slouch herself when it came to secret smiles and meanings withheld, claimed that Woolf would often say the most dreadful things about people in private. "Of course", she remarked, "one does oneself. But one doesn't expect it of Virginia Woolf." One can think of no higher praise than to say that what one doesn't expect of Woolf, one absolutely expects of Austen. The tone of Austen's work, perfectly controlled throughout – in *Northanger Abbey* there is that delightfully sly nod to readers in conclusion that they "will see in the tell-tale compression of the pages before them, that we are all hastening together to perfect felicity" (not); in *Persuasion* there is the acknowledgement that the happiness of Anne and Wentworth, united in marriage at last, remains nonetheless shadowed by "the dread of a future war" ("She gloried in being a sailor's wife, but she must pay the tax of quick alarm for belonging to that profession which is, if possible, more distinguished in its domestic virtues than in its national importance") – enables her always to say what can't be said without actually having to say it. It makes one grateful that there are writers who have bothered going to the bother of all that sort of bothering. Anniversaries come and go and circuses move on, but the rigmarole lasts for ever. ∎

THE NOVELS

Facts and factions

Truths, titles and political readings of novels that are often treated as something other than what their author said they were

AUTHOR: **DEVONEY LOOSER**

The word "truth" is universally acknowledged for its attachment to Jane Austen's fiction. It is not only through her brilliant (and now sadly hackneyed) opening line to *Pride and Prejudice* (1813). Austen's novels are said to traffic in true-to-life characters, in truths in miniature detail, and in moral truths. Crediting Austen with truth-making has a long history. Sir Walter Scott's historical novels achieved bestsellerdom in the 1810s – rousing Austen's mock-jealousy – but Scott also admitted envying her novels of manners. He privately lamented Austen's besting him in truth of description and sentiment.

As Scott's literary reputation has waxed and waned, the fashion for seeing Austen's fiction as factually true has also gone in and out of style. Did she write veiled historical novels, anchored to specific people, places and events, if on a smaller scale than Scott's? Some readers say yes, choosing to advance the theory that Austen produced quasi-*romans-à-clef* of English social history. These readers often search for the keys to unlock the true meanings of her fiction. Unsurprisingly, they frequently

claim to find them.

Such quests are especially amusing because Austen's writings rarely fetishize facts. Her early foray into history writing famously describes itself as the work of a partial, prejudiced and ignorant historian. Austen humorously boasts to her readers that her history will contain very few dates. Austen's later fiction, too, ridicules the value of verifiable information. In *Mansfield Park* (1814), the obnoxious, spoilt Bertram sisters declare their less privileged cousin, the novel's heroine Fanny Price, to be ignorant because she refers to the Isle of Wight as "the Island", as if there were no other. The sisters complain about Fanny's stupidity to their loathsome aunt. They brazenly tout their superior intelligence, using as evidence their former ability to recite the names of the kings of England and a few Roman emperors. It's both curious and not that these self-satisfied girls make no mention of England's queens.

"Information" is "a tricky word" in Austen, as Deidre Shauna Lynch claims in her edition of *Mansfield Park*. In a substantial footnote, Lynch argues that information in Austen's day meant

BELOW
Hip flask of Bath Gin adorned with Jane Austen's portrait

"more than the facts or data we associate with the term" but also signalled formations, as in educational processes. She suggests that the Bertram sisters' schooling shows they have been "stuffed full of the first, at the expense of the second". Facts do not an education make.

In fact, *Mansfield Park* is the Austen novel that uses the word "fact" most frequently among her books. It crops up twenty-four times, according to *A Concordance to the Works of Jane Austen* (1982), followed closely by *Emma*'s twenty-three. Especially in *Mansfield Park*, the word "fact" appears at moments encouraging readers to be sceptical of the supposedly true. The novel's first use of "fact" is from Aunt Norris, who tries to convince her brother-in-law, Sir Thomas Bertram, that raising opposite-sex cousins under the same roof "is, in fact, the only sure way" to prevent their marrying later. The novel proves her wrong.

One of Austen's most amusing lines on the subject of truth and falsity appears in her early novella, *Lady Susan*. As the titular widow's web of lies is exposed, her female confidante

declares in sympathetic defeat, "Facts are such horrid things". It is difficult not to imagine the self-satisfied chuckle of a fiction writer crafting this line. Yet any conjuring of Austen's chuckle here is precisely that – imagined.

Given Austen's unapologetic acknowledgement that her own stories are fabricated, it is also amusing how often we seek to yoke them to actualities. She subtitled the fiction published during her lifetime with "A Novel", despite other labels available to her. Authors of prose fiction from the period used story, romance, tale, "founded on facts", or sometimes no subtitle at all. Titles, too, could be slippery. One novelist invited readers to supply their own: *Read, and Give It a Name: A novel* (1813) by Mrs Llewellyn. (A cutting reviewer opined, "Be it named – 'MEDIOCRITY!'") Austen was deliberate in delivering fictions packaged as fiction: *Pride and Prejudice: A novel. Sense and Sensibility: A novel. Mansfield Park: A novel. Emma: A novel.* This is not protesting too much, but clarity.

We have been less fastidious in labelling works derived from hers. The boundaries between fact and fiction in Austen-inspired books are strikingly porous. To take a recent example, Helena Kelly's *Jane Austen, the Secret Radical* more often resembles a novel, offering readers a copious amount of what Kelly herself dubs "truthful fictions". By contrast, the edition of Austen's novel, Lynch's annotated *Mansfield Park*, has been amplified into a significant work of criticism, mostly contained in its jumbo side margins. To make this turnabout even stranger, it is Kelly's novelish critical work that employs the bombastic rhetoric of right and wrong, while Lynch's edition gives us, within its helpful concatenation of facts, a more reasonable number of mights and perhaps.

No fewer than ten recent Austen-inspired books feature the word "secret", with the criticism not always easily differentiated from the fiction. *Social Jane: The small, secret sociology of Jane Austen* (2013) is clearly telegraphed as criticism, and *Jane Austen Stole My Boyfriend: A secret diary* (2011) is unquestionably a novel. But what about *Jane Austen, or The Secret of Style* (2003) versus *Jane Fairfax: The secret of the second heroine in Jane Austen's "Emma"* (1991)? If you guessed that the former is packaged as literary criticism and the latter as fiction, then you're no dull elf.

The keywords real, true/truth, and mystery/mysterious present less prevalent but similarly resonant patterns in today's Austen book titles. It may be another unacknowledged harking back to the novel's earlier history, which gave us *Very Strange, but Very True!: Or, the history of an old man's young wife* (1803) by the prolific novelist Francis Lathom. Lathom is best known as the author of *The Midnight Bell* (1798), one of the five horrid novels referenced in Austen's *Northanger Abbey* (1818). He also penned *Mystery: A novel* (1800), *Astonishment!!!: A romance of a century ago* (1802) and *The Impenetrable Secret, Find it Out!: A novel* (1805). That last title was so catchy that it was echoed in a more logical version by Mrs Meeke, in *There Is a Secret, Find it Out!: A novel* (1808). Elizabeth Meeke, a very prolific novelist, was recently identified by Simon Macdonald as the stepsister of the famed novelist Frances Burney.

But today's factish-fictiony Austen books go beyond titles. Editions sold as annotated Austens – melding her fiction with bonus details, visuals and interpretations in the tradition of the extra-illustrated book – have also become quite popular. The affordable Penguin Random House print paperback editions, with material by David M. Shapard, seem destined for general sales, as well as for classrooms. The publisher used its annotated *Pride and Prejudice* as the basis for an innovative and award-winning iTunes Interactive Edition. It features thousands of notes, illustrations, maps, timelines, quizzes and generous video content, including interviews with contemporary critics and novelists and clips from BBC adaptations, for less than £10. (Disclosure: I am one of the edition's talking heads.) In Lynch's *Mansfield Park* edition, you may study charts of the Royal Navy's organization, peruse fashion plates and scrutinize playbills, featured among the edition's 117 well-chosen illustrations. You might read about Antigua, bonnets, commons, duties, Edgeworth and freeholds. Lynch is clear about her methods of selection for the material. She set out to "make Austen's engagements with the debates of the period visible to a twenty-first century audience, so that they may draw their own conclusions about Austen's meanings". Lynch regularly highlights controversy in *Mansfield Park*, in an edition with more show than tell, which refuses to talk down to its readers.

Still, one wonders how most readers will approach these annotated editions. An Austen first-timer might focus on the fiction, the purported main event, merely skimming the added content on

Austen has been an icon of many political stripes, including radical and feminist, for generations

DEVONEY LOOSER

the outer margins. But a reader more experienced in Austen could do the opposite, confining his or her perusal to the added material alone, using the primary text only glancingly, as if the fiction were the footnote. In such a scenario, the original novel becomes less visible, more incidental alongside the copious notes and images.

Before we decide whether to welcome or lament the recent trend of Austen novel-cum-criticism-cum-novel, we ought to explore whether it is an innovation at all. We might suspect that our own era of post-truthiness serves as the origin of fact/fiction title-jumbling in Austen studies, but the phenomenon is hardly new. "Jane Austen's Husband" (1897) is a work of literary criticism about the poet George Crabbe, a married man whom Austen once made a joke about conjugally coveting. Non-fiction, too, are "Jane Austen's Lovers" (1889) and "Round the Clock with Jane Austen" (1923).

Austen has also been an icon of many political stripes, including radical and feminist, for generations. (If that fact surprises, it may arise from an ardour to describe Janeite history as if it starts with Colin Firth.) The early twentieth-century women's suffrage movement embraced Austen, from its non-violent to its radical branches. Many of the first playwrights, directors and actors of early Austen stage adaptations, in the 1890s and early 1900s, were or would become suffragists. Jane Austen's name was featured on a banner marched through the streets of London in a 1908 demonstration. (That banner survives in the Women's Library at the London School of Economics and Political Science.) In 1909, suffragists put Austen on stage as a character in the propaganda play *A Pageant of Great Women*. The radical Austen was your great-grandmother's Jane Austen.

But Austen's radicalism was not an invention of the early twentieth-century suffragists, either. Before that, literati in the gentlemen's club set recognized that their contemporaries had been too quick to declare the case closed on Austen's alleged apolitical conservatism. In 1890, the historian and reformer Goldwin Smith describes Austen's fiction as having "a flash of something like Radical sympathy with the oppressed governess". In 1903, William Dean Howells suggests that Austen's fiction expresses radical positions, "whether she knew it or not", because she "was in her way asserting the Rights of Man as unmistakably as the French revolutionists".

Three decades ago, Claudia L. Johnson argued for a progressive, political Austen, in her extraordinary *Jane Austen: Women, politics, and the novel* (1988). Johnson suggests Austen "was able not to depoliticize her work – for the political implications of her work [are] implicit in the subject matter itself – but rather to depolemicize it". Austen effectively advanced her liberal ideals by making them more palatable to a wide readership, forgoing divisive diatribe. Depolemical is not apolitical.

Nor was Johnson's a lone voice. An earlier book, Mary Evans's *Jane Austen and the State* (1987), goes further still, repeatedly identifying Austen's fiction as radical. Evans calls *Mansfield Park*'s Fanny Price perhaps the best character in all fiction for offering a "radical critique of bourgeois patriarchy, its norms, and values of behaviour". Deidre Shauna Lynch echoes this argument when she writes that *Mansfield Park* offers "shrewd analyses of the power politics of domestic life". In the case of *Mansfield Park*, critical debates have been incendiary and divisive. Since Edward Said's reading of Austen as silently endorsing slavery in *Culture and Imperialism* (1991), *Mansfield Park*

has become a flash-point in studies of colonialism. For Helena Kelly, "*Mansfield Park* is about slavery", from start to finish. Lynch sees less one-to-one correspondence. Both, however, express indebtedness for their interpretations to Paula Byrne's excellent historicization of Amma Asante's film *Belle* (2013), another notable moment in the history of Austen-inspired "facting" of fiction.

Byrne's book, also called *Belle*, pieces together a fascinating account of Dido Elizabeth Belle, a real-life, mixed-race eighteenth-century woman. Her father figure and great-uncle was the Earl of Mansfield, Lord Chief Justice, famous for his 1772 ruling, said to have made slavery illegal in England. The question for critics is what we are supposed to do with Austen's use of the word "Mansfield" in *Mansfield Park*. Is Lord Mansfield being "name-checked" by Austen, as Lynch puts it? Is Austen's use of the name Mansfield in her novel's title an inspiration and an invitation to conjecture, as Lynch would have it, or a solvable political puzzle pointing to radicalism, as Kelly would?

If we claim Austen for radicalism, whether conjecturally or with confidence, we are joining a longstanding popular and critical trend. Lynch argues in her *Mansfield Park* edition that Austen was a "social commentator" on "imperial policy" and "class and sectarian strife". Nevertheless, Lynch does not give us an author who offers a social formula or political answers. Austen wasn't writing treatises. Lynch notes that in reading *Mansfield Park* it is "hard to get your bearings". She quotes Bharat Tandon on Austen's "power to frustrate". Perhaps seeking truths – political and otherwise – in Austen's fiction means thinking more deeply about the preposterous fact that so many read these novels in order to come to right answers. ■

THE NOVELS

The Silence of the Bertrams

Slavery and what chronology means to a controversy surrounding *Mansfield Park*

AUTHOR: **BRIAN SOUTHAM**

"Did not you hear me ask him about the slave trade last night?" "I did – and was in hopes the question would be followed up by others. It would have pleased your uncle to be inquired of farther."

"And I longed to do it – but there was such a dead silence!"

Lionel Trilling's 1954 essay on *Mansfield Park* has played an important part in shaping modern opinion of the novel, in helping to define its greatness and to identify what Trilling termed "its power to offend". Trilling had much to say about the significance for Jane Austen of "profession" and "duty", and why the amateur theatricals in the Bertram household were regarded as so reprehensible. Forty years on, attention has returned to *Mansfield Park* in a way which Trilling would never have anticipated, "its power to offend" now overshadowed by a different power. Recent accounts (by Edward Said, for example) have placed the novel in the canon of colonial fiction, with slavery, literal and metaphorical, at its heart. This line of interpretation, which seems likely to become established, is distinctively and ambitiously historical.

Its plausibility depends very considerably upon the accurate dating of events within the novel and in the world contemporary with its story. Unfortunately, to everyone's disadvantage, despite much guesswork and many calculations, the chronology of *Mansfield Park* remains an area of misunderstanding. Equally, there is general misunderstanding about the circumstances of the slave trade and its abolition, an issue central to the slavery/colonial approach; and without a firm historical base, any attempt at historical interpretation is liable to run aground.

But when we return to the text, we find that this confusion is entirely needless. We are able to pinpoint the course of events, not from the vague "About thirty years ago" of the opening, which is no more than a glance backwards at the antecedents of the story proper, but from a single reference in Chapter Sixteen, the chapter in which Edmund visits Fanny in the East room seeking her approval for taking the part of Anhalt in *Lovers' Vows*. On the table are some books, "her books of which she had been a collector from the first hour of her commanding a

BELOW
Fanny and Edmund
in *Mansfield Park*

shilling". Edmund looks at three of them: *Macartney's Journal of the Embassy to China* (1807), Johnson's *Idler* and Crabbe's *Tales* (in full, *Tales in Verse*), published in September 1812. In the next chapter, Sir Thomas surprises the household with his sudden and unannounced return from Antigua. In the strained atmosphere of the family gathering that follows, Tom tries to delay his father's discovery of their rehearsing *Lovers' Vows* and rattles on about the pheasant-shooting and the wretched weather they have been having that October.

So Jane Austen fixes the month and year of Sir Thomas's return as October 1812. October 1813 is theoretically possible, until we calculate that this would put the end of the story at mid-1814, about nine months after Austen had completed the novel; and it is highly improbable that she would use a time-scheme setting the final section of the story in the future. With October 1812 as the known point, the reader can work backwards and forwards in the story to construct a time-scheme for the main action of just under three years, within which fall six key events: Sir

Thomas and Tom leave for Antigua about October 1810; Tom returns about September 1811; Sir Thomas writes home, April 1812; Fanny in possession of Crabbe's *Tales*, published September 1812; Sir Thomas returns, late October 1812; Edmund turns to Fanny, summer 1813.

The 1810–13 chronology makes sense in every way; and it provides the right slot for Tom's reference, in September 1812, to the "strange business" in America, ie, what he would have read and heard by now about the outbreak and early events of the Anglo-American War a "strange business" because the United States declared war on Britain on June 16, unaware that Britain had already dropped the Orders in Council which restricted American trade with Europe and authorized the searching of American ships for British deserters, the cause of the dispute.

To confirm the novel's chronology is not simply a pedantic exercise. With the advent of slave and colonialist perspectives, the dating of the story becomes important to our understanding of *Mansfield Park*, since the Bertrams are financed by

the income from their Antigua estate and Sir Thomas takes his journey there in an attempt to halt its decline – successfully, as it turns out. Although these circumstances play a significant part in the first half of the story and resonate throughout the novel, traditional accounts of *Mansfield Park* have ignored the purpose of Sir Thomas's voyage (some describe it, using Austen's own word, as merely a visit on "business") and have treated the journey as no more than a device to get the head of the family out of the way and allow the young people to run wild. But to accept the historical force of Austen's portrait is to view Sir Thomas not just as a patriarchal English country gentleman but also in his "colonial" role as an absentee plantation owner, in Parliament an active member of the West Indian lobby, now compelled by "some recent losses on his West Indian Estate" to return to Antigua and (as we may suppose) take over the running of the plantation from the resident manager and restore it to prosperity. "Fat managers and lean employees" was the uncomfortable adage current on the island.

A variety of datings has been proposed for the action of the novel, some of which open up wholly misleading lines of interpretation: 1803–6 or 1805–7 sets Sir Thomas's visit just ahead of the abolition of the slave trade in 1807; whereas 1808–9 or 1808–10 give us post-abolitionist readings. Equally, in Chapter Twenty-One, Fanny's "slave trade" question to Sir Thomas carried a very different significance in 1812 than it would if asked in earlier years. It was a question which Fanny wanted to follow up with others. But she was deterred from doing so by the "dead silence" that followed, her cousins "sitting by without speaking a word, or seeming at all interested in the subject". We are left to wonder about Sir Thomas's reply. Charitably, we can suppose that he answers Fanny fully and to her satisfaction. But Jane Austen glides over the point, leaving it wholly unresolved, perhaps even weighing the balance against him. A moment earlier, Fanny has been telling Edmund how she loves to hear Sir Thomas talking of the West Indies, how she "could listen to him for an hour together. It entertains me more than many other things have done." Earlier, Sir Thomas was "communicative and chatty . . . as to his voyage". Now, the "dead silence" hints that his loquacity may have dried up at the mention of slaves. As if to underline the point, Austen later restores Sir Thomas's animation when he comes to talk to William Price about "the balls of Antigua", a recreation that the young midshipman may also have enjoyed on his West Indies tour of duty.

The precise interpretation of this scene – of Fanny's questions, asked and unasked, of the "dead silence", of the cousins' "seeming" absence of interest – turns crucially on the issue of dating. Some critics fasten immediately on Fanny's reference to the slave trade and conclude, over-hastily, that her question to Sir Thomas must have been put before the Abolition Act became law in March 1807. But this is to misunderstand the historical situation. The Act came into force in two stages: from May 1, 1807, no ship with slaves on board was permitted to sail from any port in the British Empire unless legally cleared before that date; and from March 1, 1808, no slaves were to be landed. By the letter of the Act, for Britain and its overseas possessions, the slave trade was ended: "hereby utterly abolished, prohibited, and declared to be unlawful". Declaration, of course, is one thing, enforcement another. This branch of commerce, recognized, sanctioned and encouraged for 250 years, now went underground.

It was a trade that the African patrol was unable to stop. The naval presence was laughable: two elderly vessels, a frigate and a sloop, facing the slave outlets along 3,000 miles of coastline, and behind them the vast extent of the Atlantic sea lanes. Four more ships were added to the patrol in 1810, to some immediate effect. But deterrent policing was only possible years later, when the Navy was clear of its involvement in the

American and Napoleonic wars and when the Admiralty, for centuries protector of the Islands, was sufficiently persuaded of the abolitionist cause to enforce the blockade wholeheartedly. A further immediate weakness lay with the Act itself, since trading was treated there as a contraband activity and carried penalties no heavier than confiscation and fines. Punitive as these costs could be, profits were so high that traders were prepared to risk capture. Even when losing two out of three of their ships and human cargoes, they could still come out with a profit. Four years later, in 1811, in an attempt to clamp down on the continuing traffic, the Slave Trade Felony Act was introduced. This made trading a crime, carrying a penalty of up to fourteen years' transportation. Its net was cast wide, applying to British subjects trading anywhere in the world and to traders of any nationality operating within the British Empire. In part, this was directed at British slave-dealers trading under neutral flags of convenience. This was a device

ABOVE
William Clark's depiction of slaves working on a plantation in Antigua, 1823

employed well before 1807 and used by traders to avoid the Acts of 1789 and 1799 regulating the number of slaves according to the ship's weight and dimensions, humanitarian measures which cut into their profits. The Felony Act closed further loopholes and increased existing penalties. The severity of these measures had some effect. But since the demand remained "buying is cheaper than breeding" was a mainstay of planter wisdom - the trade persisted.

As a further step, the abolitionists then persuaded the government to introduce the compulsory registration of slaves, beginning with Trinidad, under an Order in Council of March 1812. The registration, conducted in 1813, seemed to make their point. The returns indicated a sharp growth in the slave population from just over 21,000, as recorded in a recent census, to almost 26,000. The abolitionists were also concerned by the increasing traffic of other countries. Supported by British capital, Spain and Portugal were trading actively; and the United States was to maintain a flourishing trade right up to the Civil War. The Africa Institution was established immediately after the 1807 Act to "promote" the "civilization and happiness" of Africans, and "the abolition of the African Slave Trade by Foreign powers". Almost at once, however, it was forced by events to turn its energies to breaches of the British abolition, while the foreign trade and Africa took second place.

So when Fanny ventured to put her question to the slave-owning Sir Thomas in October 1812 – the date Austen so evidently signals to us – the "slave trade" was still a burning issue, a persistent and horrifying scandal, debated in Parliament and extensively reported and discussed in the newspapers and periodicals. Pamphlets describing "recent slave trade atrocities" continued to circulate, and abolitionists voiced their indignation and repugnance even more vehemently. The campaign was also waged in the periodical press, notably in the *Edinburgh Review*, urging the strict application of the Abolition and Felony Acts and ensuring that the public was informed of slave atrocities in the West Indies and elsewhere. Appalling as conditions had been on the slave-ships before abolition, totally unregulated they were now even worse.

The planter cause was carried in the *Quarterly Review*, founded in 1809, and in pamphlets which revived all

Austen did not have to look far. The slave connection was in the immediate history of her own family

BRIAN SOUTHAM

the old arguments in defence: for the benefits it conferred upon the Africans, for the fulfilment of Gospel precepts, for the support of a West Indian commerce essential to the mother country. This is the pressure of history on *Mansfield Park*. It enables us to understand why the "traffic in human flesh" (the abolitionist term, which Austen later uses in *Emma*) was a sensitive subject, unmentionable in the home of Sir Thomas Bertram; and unmentioned, too, until Fanny was courageous enough to raise it, a breaking of the taboo met instantly with a confounding "dead silence".

For the characters and circumstances of her story, Jane Austen did not have to look far. The slave connection was to be found in the immediate history of her own family. In 1760, Jane's father, the Revd George Austen, was appointed principal trustee of a plantation in Antigua, a fact unmentioned in the family biographies and memoirs. During Jane Austen's lifetime, the full abomination of slavery struck the nation's conscience and the "harshness and despotism" of the plantation owners and their managers were reported back to the family by Francis Austen from his experience of naval duty in the West Indies. A silence not unlike the "dead silence" at Mansfield Park may have begun to gather over Mr Austen's West Indian connections – connections which extended deeper into the household. The owner of the Antigua plantation, James Langford Nibbs, a former pupil of Mr Austen at Oxford, stood in 1765 as godfather for James, the eldest Austen son. Like Sir Thomas Bertram, Mr Nibbs had a spendthrift elder son, James junior; and like Tom Bertram, James junior was taken off to Antigua by his father to detach him from his "unwholesome connections". In this circuitous way, the Austens too had a

dependence, however slight, upon the prosperity of a plantation in Antigua; and events similar to the *Mansfield Park* story would have become known to Jane Austen in her childhood. Like many planters' sons, James Langford Nibbs was sent home from the West Indies for education and gentrification. He aimed to set himself up as a propertied English gentleman, and began the process with a grant of arms in 1759, crowning the elevation of the Nibbs family with a country seat in Devon, where he died in 1795. Could this be the story, typical of West Indian advancement in the mother country, that Jane Austen drew on in portraying the Bertrams in their "modern-built house"? There is something distinctly "modern-built", nouveau and West Indian about Sir Thomas and his social standing, a point worth making since some commentators wholly misplace Sir Thomas, writing about him as a member of the old and established landed gentry who bears an ancient title. It is not only Mr Rushworth's £12,000 a year and his large estate that make him such a catch for Maria: "It was a connection exactly of the right sort", an "alliance" with the old-established gentry, the Rushworths having lived for centuries in "their ancient manorial residence", "a marriage which could bring" Sir Thomas "such an addition of respectability and influence".

Alerted at the very opening of the story to Sir Thomas's overseas interests, his "West Indian property", Jane Austen's readers would recognize his type immediately: not at all the character "West-Injine" fresh from the Caribbean – vulgar, flamboyant, free-spending and high-living – sneered at by the King, the court and the Tory gentry, the detestation of Cobbett and the delight of satirists from Hogarth and Smollett onwards but a Mr Nibbs, a

second-generation absentee, set on rising above and obscuring the origins of his wealth; on giving his sons, via Eton and Oxford, connections and a gentleman's education; and on securing further connections and alliances through the marriage of his daughters, and through the marriage of Fanny Price to Henry Crawford. Students of patronage will also understand Sir Thomas's doubts whether his influence will run as far as obtaining a commission for Fanny's midshipman brother. In 1812, with the economic importance of the West Indies in decline, the extent of Sir Thomas's "interest" was in decline too. The portrait is subtle, deeply grounded in observation, and to see Sir Thomas in this character helps us to follow what part the Antiguan associations have to play in the comedy and in the darker side of *Mansfield Park*.

When Nabokov was preparing his lecture on *Mansfield Park* given to American students in the 1940s and 50s, he drew maps of England, marking the towns and counties mentioned in the story and tracing out the routes and distances travelled by the characters. He made plans of the rooms of Mansfield Park and the dozen or so areas Jane Austen specifies in her description of the gardens and grounds at Sotherton. And he laid out an extensive (if incorrect) chronology of the story itself. All this, Nabokov claimed, was the "exact information about details, about such combinations of details as yield the sensual spark without which a book is dead". It was the compilation of this "exact information" which led him to describe his course of lectures as "a kind of detective investigation of the mystery of literary structures". The true chronology of the story is surely one of the items of "exact information" which can yield a vital clue in the

"investigation" of *Mansfield Park* and lead the reader towards the penetration of its "mystery".

Edward Said gives us an Austen world of altogether different dimensions. In *Culture and Imperialism*, he views *Mansfield Park* in a global perspective, embracing the Mediterranean and India as well as the Caribbean, locating the house itself "at the centre of an arc of interests and concerns spanning the hemisphere, two major seas and four continents". It is a wide and exciting prospect, as stimulating as Nabokov's loving attention to fine detail, inviting us to consider *Mansfield Park* in the colonial aspect of its world setting. Physical and commercial geography here go hand-in-hand with moral geography.

Between the household of Mansfield Park and the plantation on Antigua, Said finds a relaxed and balanced articulation: "What assures the domestic tranquillity and attractive harmony of one is the productivity and regulated discipline of the other". Not only the household, including Fanny Price, but Austen too, can contemplate Antigua with satisfaction as a sustaining and uncontaminated source of well-being: "for them the island is wealth, which Austen regards as being converted to propriety, order and, at the end of the novel, comfort, an added good". This conjunction of moral and material benefit finds the author at one with her creations: an alignment which joins Sir Thomas, Fanny and Jane Austen:

References to Sir Thomas Bertram's overseas possessions are threaded through; they give him his wealth, occasion his absences, fix his social status at home and abroad, and make possible his values, to which Fanny Price (and Austen herself) finally subscribes. If this is a novel about "ordination", as Austen says, the right to

colonial possessions helps directly to establish social order and moral priorities at home.

Professor Said's formulations are elegant and beguiling, seeming to lay bare the "colonial" mechanism and process of the novel, the dynamic of its certainties and authority. In this telling exposition, *Culture and Imperialism* carries a challenging and commanding thesis, which may well prove to be as influential as Trilling's. If so, there is a no less pressing case for attending to the letter of the text, for dating the story correctly, and for taking account of the circumstances that stand behind the scene in Chapter Twenty-One where Fanny puts her "slave trade" question and "dead silence" prevails. Fanny gets no reply to her forbidden question because none is possible from a man who has supported the slave trade as a buyer of slaves – lawfully in times past, or even illegally since 1808 – and whose own fortunes have depended on it. One of the West Indian lobby, Sir Thomas would have argued and voted for the trade's continuation over the twenty years that Abolition was contested at Westminster. History is against him. The gap of "silence" between his slave-owning "values" and those of Fanny, the sole questioner of those "values", could not be more effectively shown.

Where does Jane Austen stand in this? With Sir Thomas, as Said believes? Or with her heroine? Readers of the novel will decide for themselves. But the logic of history, biography and the text itself places Austen beside Fanny Price. *Mansfield Park*'s "power to offend" is not, as Said would have us believe, to render Fanny Price (and her creator) friends of the plantocracy. At this notable moment, in the lion's den, Fanny is unmistakably a "friend of the abolition", and Austen's readers in 1814 would have applauded the heroine and her author for exactly that. ∎

Mansfield Park

volume 1, chapter 9

"Oh! I know nothing of your furlongs, but I am sure it is a very long wood;
and that we have been winding in and out ever since we came into it;
and therefore when I say that we have walked a mile in it, I must speak within compass."
"We have been exactly a quarter of an hour here", said Edmund, taking out his watch.
"Do you think we are walking four miles an hour?"
"Oh! do not attack me with your watch. A watch is always too fast or too slow.
I cannot be dictated to by a watch."

---

*Published in 1814, Mansfield Park is often thought the most serious and substantial
of Jane Austen's novels, with a heroine, Fanny Price, whom Kingsley Amis regarded as
"morally detestable". Its artistry, however, is superb – from the lengthy sequence
about putting on a private theatrical performance to its touching,
controversially, on the question of slavery.*

ILLUSTRATION: **DARREN SMITH**

Beyond the Novels

BEYOND THE NOVELS

To the letter

In his only review for the *TLS*, a major English novelist of the twentieth century considers the correspondence of his illustrious predecessor, as edited afresh by the leading Jane Austen scholar of the day

AUTHOR: **E. M. FORSTER**

Miss Austen had no idea of what awaited Jane Austen. Within certain limits she could perhaps forecast her contemporary's future; she must have known that the novels would remain before the public for some years, and she would not have been surprised by the tributes of the Austen Leighs and of Lord Brabourne, for they were relatives, and might be expected to do what they could for an aunt. But that the affair should go farther, that it should reach the twentieth century and reach it in such proportions of that she could have had no premonition. She would have been amazed at Mr Chapman's magnificent and scholarly edition of the novels, published nine years ago, and still more amazed at the interest shown over "Love and Freindship" (*sic*) and "Sanditon", and the lid (for now we must be as modern as we can) the lid would have been put on by this final achievement of Mr Chapman's, this monumental and definitive edition of the letters.

What would she have thought about it all? The question is not uninteresting, though it is more important that we should think about it correctly ourselves, that we should maintain critical perspective, that we should not overwhelm by our superior awareness, and that Jane Austen, whom we know so well, should not distort or overshadow Miss Austen, whom we cannot know, because she died over a century ago at Winchester. Sitting up in our thousands and taking notice, as we shall, we had better first of all listen to the words of Cassandra, who was with her at the end:

I *have* lost such a Sister, such a friend as never can have been surpassed – she was the sun of my life, the gilder of every pleasure, the soother of every sorrow, I had not a thought concealed from her, and it is as if I had lost a part of myself.

We like these words of Cassandra's, and we had better read the words that follow, which we may not like so well:

I loved her only too well, not better than she deserved, but I am conscious that my affection for her made me sometimes unjust to & negligent of others, & I can acknowledge, more than as a general principle, the justice of the hand that struck the blow.

In that union of tenderness and sanctimoniousness, let us leave her for a moment to rest. She wrote letters. They have reappeared exactly as she wrote them, but in a setting which makes them look strange to her, and we are part of the setting. They do not draw distant ages together, like the letters which were written at the same time by Keats. They were temporary and local in their appeal, and their essential meaning went down with her into the grave.

Now let us honour Mr Chapman's edition. It is elaborate, but, as we may expect from a scholar of his experience and taste, he makes us search for his learning. The letters are printed without comment, and at the end of each volume we find, if we choose, an abundance of notes and other apparatus, together with illustrations which evoke the facts or the spirit of the period. The text of the letters, apparently as simple as a rectory garden, covers many little secrets, some of them only known to the children and the servants, others almost peculiar to the hens; and all are here patiently disinterred by the editor, while we look

on with admiration, our hands folded uselessly before us. For instance, when Miss Austen says: "If there were but a coach from Hungerford to Chawton!" we do not guess what lay beneath her wish, and as a matter of fact there was not very much; still there was something, and we can find out what it is by referring to the terminal note:

Caroline Austen's *Reminiscences* show that Mrs. James Austen and C. E. A. took Caroline to Cheltenham via Kintbury, there picking up Mary Jane Fowle. In their return they left M. J. F. at Kintbury and then diverged, Mrs. J. A. returning to Steventon, C. E. A. taking Caroline to Chawton. J. A.'s sigh for a coach from Hungerford is no doubt connected with this division of the party.

Erudition can no further go, and we fling up our hands in amazement as far as they will go in 1932. "How shall we ever recollect half the dishes for grandmamma?" cried Miss Bates at the Highbury Assembly Rooms: but Mr. Chapman can recollect them all, and grandmamma, the world crashing about her ears, may regale herself upon no fewer than eight indexes, one of which distinguishes the various generations of the Austen family by four types of print – namely, AUSTEN, AUSTEN, Austen and Austen.

The tact and good temper of the editing are as admirable as its learning. Naturally when one invests in a concern one comes to value it, and Mr Chapman is not exempt from this sensible rule. He has contended with the subject manfully, like St Paul at Ephesus; and would he have done so if it was not worthwhile? He puts his plea endearingly, he does not thrust his struggle down our throats, and he leads us with just the right combination of honesty and circumspection past a very dubious spot in the rectory garden. What's

wrong in the garden? The drainage? No. The novels are good – of that there is no doubt, and they are so good that everything connected with the novelist and everything she wrote ought certainly to be published and annotated. Of that, too, there is no doubt, and this elaborate edition is thoroughly justified. But – and here comes the dubious spot – are the letters themselves good? Very reluctantly, and in spite of Mr Chapman's quiet instigations to the contrary, one must answer "No".

Oh yes, one can safeguard oneself against the Janeites, should they attack. Oh yes, some of the letters are good, most of them contain something good, Cassandra may have burnt the best, Cassandra, as Mr Chapman himself conjectures, may not have been an inspiring correspondent, and nearly all the letters are addressed to Cassandra. One can qualify the unfavourable verdict this way and that, but the verdict remains. Are not most of these two volumes catalogues of trivialities which do not come alive? They were alive at the time, but they have not the magic that outlasts ink: they are the letters of Miss Austen, not of Jane Austen: and Miss Austen would think us silly to read them, for she knows that we have not and cannot have their key. When the breath left her body it was lost, though a ghost of it lingered for a time in the hands of those who had loved her. Cassandra understood, her niece Fanny Knight understood, the Austen Leighs and Lord Brabourne had some conception – but we students of today, unrelated to her by blood, what part have we in this family talk, and whose triviality do we expose but our own?

It would be incorrect to say that the letters do not suggest the novels. They suggest them constantly: the quiet houses, the miry lanes, the

▬▬
BELOW
Fanny Knight, later Lady Knatchbull (1793–1882), one of Austen's nieces

conundrums, the absence of the very rich and the very poor, the snobbery which flourishes where distinctions of incomes are slight – all are present, and some of the characters are also present in solution. But never the finer characters. These never seem to get uppermost when Miss Austen writes a letter. They belong to another part of her mind. Neither Emma Woodhouse nor Anne Elliot nor even Frank Churchill or Mary Crawford dominates her pen. The controls are rather Lydia Bennet, Mrs Jennings and Sir Thomas Bertram, a bizarre and inauspicious combine. In the earlier letters Lydia Bennet is all pervading; balls, officers, giggling, dresses, officers, balls, fill sheet after sheet until everyone except Kitty grows weary. Nothing came of it. Nothing could have come of it except a husband. It has none of the disinterested rapture which fills Catherine Morland in the pump room at Bath, or Natasha Rostov in the far-distant universe of *War and Peace*, dancing the polonaise, dancing, dancing, because she is young. The young girl dances here and her eyes sparkle duly, but they are observant and hard; officers, dresses, officers, giggling, balls, and it is no wonder that a hostile critic (Miss Mitford) should compare her at once to a poker and to a butterfly. And when Lydia Bennet retires we may catch the tread of Mrs Jennings, and that eighteenth-century frankness of hers which has somehow strayed into too small a room and become unacceptable. In the novels, how well advised was the authoress of *Sense and Sensibility* to become a prude, and to curtail in its second edition the reference to a natural daughter! In the letters, how Miss Austen's occasional comments on expectant motherhood do jar! She faces the facts, but they are not her facts, and her lapses of taste over carnality can be deplorable, no doubt because they arise from lack of

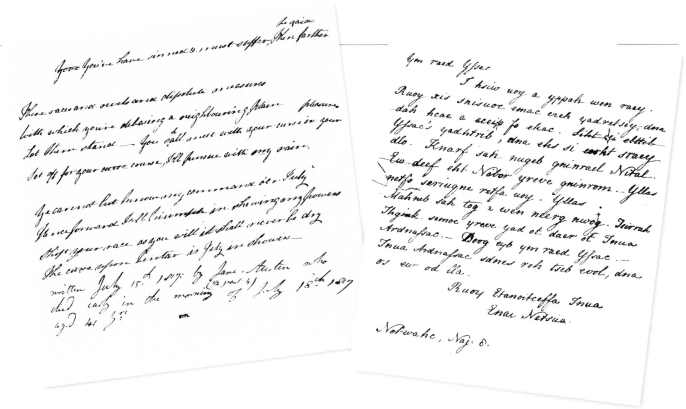

feeling. She can write, for instance, and write it as a jolly joke, that "Mrs. Hall of Sherborne was brought to bed yesterday of a dead child, some weeks before she expected, owing to a fright. I suppose she happened unawares to look at her husband". Did Cassandra laugh? Probably, but all that we catch at this distance is the whinneying of harpies.

And then we come to the serious moments. Mrs Jennings follows Lydia Bennet and Sir Thomas Bertram takes the stage, unapproachable, uncontrovertible. Listen how his spirit, though not his style, sums up the merits and demerits of Sir John Moore:

I am sorry to find that Sir J. Moore has a mother living, but tho' a very Heroick son, he might not be a very necessary one to her happiness. – Deacon Morrell may be more to Mrs. Morrell. – I wish Sir John had united something of the Christian with the Hero in his death.

The accidents of birth and relationship were more sacred to her than anything else in the world

E. M. FORSTER

And when an intimate sorrow comes (the death of her own father) she yields to formalism and writes: "Your mind will already forestall the sort of event which I have to communicate. Our dear Father has closed his virtuous & happy life, in a death almost as free from suffering as his Children could have wished". It is adequate – Sir Thomas Bertram is always that: but it gives no freedom to the heart, it has none of the outpour which we found in that letter quoted above from Cassandra.

Triviality, varied by touches of ill breeding and of sententiousness, characterizes these letters as a whole, particularly the earlier letters; and certain critics of weight, Mr Chapman among them, find the triviality delightful, and rightly point out that there is a charm in little things. Yes, when it is the charm of Cowper. But the little things must hold out their little hands to one another; and here there is a scrappiness which prevents even tartness from telling. This brings us to the heart of the matter, to Miss Austen's fundamental weakness as a letter-writer. She has not enough subject-matter on which to exercise her powers. Her character and sex as well as her environment removed her from public affairs, and she was too sincere and spontaneous to affect any interest which she did not feel. She takes no account of politics or religion,

and none of the war except when it brings prize-money to her brothers. Her comments on literature are provincial and perfunctory – with one exception, and a significant one, which we shall cite in a moment. When she writes a letter she has nothing in her mind except the wish to tell her sister everything; and so she flits from the cows lo the currant bushes, from the currant bushes to Mrs Hall of Sherborne, gives Mrs Hall a tap, and flits back again. She suffers from a poverty of material which did no injury to the novels, and indeed contributes to their triumph. Miss Bates may flit and Mrs Norris tap as much as they like, because they do so inside a frame which has been provided by a great artist, and Merylon may reproduce the atmosphere of Steventon because it imports something else – some alignment not to be found on any map. The letters lack direction. What an improvement when she is startled, an elm falls, they have to go to the dentist! Then her powers of description find fuller play, and to the affection which she always feels for her correspondents she adds concentration, and an interest in the subject matter.

The improvement becomes more noticeable in the second volume, that is to say after 1811. She had received a series of pleasant surprises. Her novels, which had always found favour in private readings, began to get published and gain wider audiences. Warren Hastings admired them, and *Emma* was dedicated to the Prince Regent shortly after his victory at Waterloo. She went to London oftener, perhaps saw Mr Crabbe in the distance, and had a note from Mrs Hannah More. While rating these joys at their proper worth, she could not but gain the notion of a more amusing and varied world; and perhaps she is one of the few country writers whom wider experience and consort with the literary would not have ruined.

Meanwhile her success reacted on her family. Her seven brothers (with the exception of a mysterious George who is never mentioned), her sister, her sisters-in-law, her nephews and, most of all, her nieces were deeply impressed. One of the nieces, Anna, took to scribbling on her own, and sent Aunt Jane from time to time instalments of a novel to read aloud to Aunt Cassandra. Miss Austen's replies are admirable. She is stimulated because the writer is a relation, and she pours out helpful criticisms, all put in a kindly, easy way. Most of them are connected with "getting things right" – always a preoccupation with English novelists, from Defoe to Arnold Bennett. Times, places and probabilities must be considered, but Anna must beware of copying life slavishly, for life sometimes gets things wrong:

I have scratched out Sir Thos: from walking with the other Men to the Stables &ct the very day after breaking his arm – for though I find your Papa did walk out immediately after his arm was set, I think it can be so little usual as to *appear* unnatural in a book – & it does not seem to be material that Sir Thos: should go with them. – Lyme will not do. Lyme is towards 40 miles distant from Dawlish & would not be talked

of there. – I have put Starcross instead. If you prefer *Exeter*, that must be always safe.

Thursday. We finished it last night, after our return from drinking tea at the Gt House. – The last chapter does not please us so well, we do not thoroughly like the *Play*: perhaps from having had too much of Plays in that way lately. And we think you had better not leave England. Let the Portmans go to Ireland, but as you know nothing of the Manners there you had better not go with them. You will be in danger of giving false representations. Stick to Bath and the Foresters. There you will be quite at home. – Your Aunt C. does not like desultory novels and is rather fearful yours will be too much so, that there will be too frequently a change from one set of people to another, & that circumstances will be sometimes introduced of apparent consequence, which will lead to nothing. – It will not be so great an objection to *me*, if it does. I allow much more Latitude than she does – & think Nature and Spirit cover many sins of a wandering story.

Here, again, the English school of fiction speaks, and puts its case amiably and privately, as it should. Manifestos belong to abroad. Aunt Cassandra likes a book to be neat and tidy: Aunt Jane does not much mind. And Anna, receiving these letters, in which detailed comment is mixed with sound generalizations, must have been delighted; she must have found her novel much better than she thought and yet been stimulated to correct in it what was wrong. We share the enthusiasm. It sounds a lovely novel, and we turn to the terminal notes to see what more Mr. Chapman has to tell us about it. Alas; he can tell us too much:

The story to which most of these letters of Aunt Jane's refer was never finished. It was laid aside because my mother's hands were so full . . . . The story was laid by for years, and then one day in a fit of despondency burnt. I

BELOW
The Prince Regent, later George IV, to whom Austen dedicated *Emma*

remember sitting on the rug and watching its destruction, amused with the flames and the sparks which kept breaking out in the blackened paper.

Thus writes Anna's daughter; and Anna's novel, with the Portmans and Foresters, who seemed so fascinating, has gone up the chimney for ever. But the tiny flicker of light which it casts backwards is valuable. We see Miss Austen and Jane Austen for a moment as one person. The letter-writer and the novelist have fused, because a letter is being written to a niece about a novel. Family feeling has done the trick; and, after all, whatever opinion we hold about her, we must agree that the supreme thing in life to her was the family. She knew no other allegiance; if there was an early love affair in the west of England, and if her lover died, as did her sister Cassandra's, she never clung to his memory, unless she utilizes it in *Persuasion*. Intimacy out of the unknown never overwhelmed her. No single person ever claimed her. She was part of a family, and her dearest Cassandra only the dearest in that family. The family was the unit within which her heart had liberty of choice; friends, neighbours, plays and fame were all objects to be picked up in the course of a flight outside and brought back to the nest for examination. They often laughed over the alien trophies, for they were a hard humorous family. And these letters, however we judge them on their own count, are invaluable as a document. They show more clearly than ever, that Miss Austen was part of the Austens, the Knights, the Leighs, the Lefroys. The accidents of birth and relationship were more sacred to her than anything else in the world, and she introduced this faith as the groundwork of her six great novels. ■

Sense and Sensibility
volume 1, chapter 16

"Have you been lately in Sussex?" said Elinor.

"I was at Norland about a month ago."

"And how does dear, dear Norland look?" cried Marianne.

"Dear, dear Norland", said Elinor, "probably looks much as it always does at this time of year.
The woods and walks thickly covered with dead leaves."

"Oh!" cried Marianne, "with what transporting sensations have I formerly seen them fall!
How have I delighted, as I walked, to see them driven in showers about me by the wind!
What feelings have they, the season, the air altogether inspired!
Now there is no one to regard them. They are seen only as nuisance,
swept hastily off, and driven as much as possible from the sight."

"It is not every one", said Elinor, "who has your passion for dead leaves."

Jane Austen's first published novel, **Sense and Sensibility**, *appeared in 1811.
It tells the story of two sisters, Elinor and Marianne Dashwood, after they are effectively
exiled with their mother from the family home (the Norland Park mentioned here);
there are depths of moral intrigue beneath the brilliant,
superficial story of romance that follows.*

ILLUSTRATION: **DARREN SMITH**

BEYOND THE NOVELS

Ungentle Jane

In praise of the violence – and irreverence – of the budding author's earliest works of fiction

AUTHOR: **PAULA BYRNE**

Edward Bond once wrote, "I write about violence as naturally as Jane Austen does about manners". Bond may be surprised to know that Austen was also interested in violence and began her writing career pushing at the boundaries of what was acceptable and tasteful in literary fiction. As Kathryn Sutherland wrote in her introduction to an edition of Austen's "juvenilia": "Jane Austen's earliest writings are violent, restless, anarchic and exuberantly expressionistic. Drunkenness, female brawling, sexual misdemeanour and murder run riot across their pages".

When I was a schoolteacher, nothing gave me more pleasure than shocking cynical teenagers by teaching Austen's early works. Without knowing the identity of the author in question, though recognizing the eighteenth-century style of the work, the students were invariably delighted by the irreverent, Monty Pythonesque absurdity of the comedy. The knowledge that this was the work of an early-teen Austen, known to them only as chronicler of the marriage plot,

increased their pleasure. As Sutherland notes, this is "laugh-out-loud" humour.

Violence can be very funny. Slapstick humour, from the moment granny slipped on a banana skin, often depends on vigorous, violent action, where people get hurt. Austen gets this. Chase scenes, collisions, crude practical jokes and horseplay are the building blocks of her slapstick. She delights in physical comedy. Her characters scuffle, drink too much, punch, kick and shove. Here she is in an early skit describing families becoming great friends: "From this period, the intimacy between the Families of Fitzroy, Drummond and Falknor, daily increased till at length it grew to such a pitch, that they did not scruple to kick one another out of the window on the slightest provocation".

Why is this so amusing? It's the physical activity of kicking, but it is also the contrast between the action and the pitch-perfect rendering of the poised Johnsonian sentence. This is why by far the most brilliant of the many modern adaptations of Austen is Seth Grahame-Smith's *Pride and Prejudice and Zombies* (2009): "As Mr Darcy walked off, Elizabeth felt her blood turn cold.

RIGHT
Poster for the film version of Seth Grahame-Smith's 2009 novel *Pride and Prejudice and Zombies* (2016)

She had never in her life been so insulted . . . . She meant to follow this proud Mr Darcy outside and open his throat". Austen would have loved the manner in which the decorum of the prose is maintained even as the action reverts to the zaniness of the juvenilia.

For the young Austen, the more absurd the plot the better. "The Beautiful Cassandra" elopes not with a handsome young stranger but with a bonnet; characters who meet one another for the first time at a formal party do not scruple to sit on one another's laps; an attractive maiden breaks her leg when she is caught in a steel man-trap set for poachers in the grounds of the gentleman she is pursuing. "Oh! Cruel Charles to wound the hearts & legs of all the fair", Lady Williams cries with a neat use of the rhetorical device of syllepsis (Austen, following her beloved Dr Johnson, would have preferred the term zeugma). This is writing that rejoices in its own cleverness.

Austen's taste for the absurd is exquisitely rendered in her command of dialogue. We meet two sisters, one beautiful and foolish; the other ugly and

clever. In this topsy-turvy world, it is the hump-backed Rebecca who garners the compliments:

Lovely and too charming Fair one, notwithstanding your forbidding Squint, your greasy tresses and your swelling Back, which are more frightful than imagination can paint or pen describe, I cannot refrain from expressing my rapture, at the Engaging Qualities of your Mind, which so amply atone for the Horror with which your first appearance must ever inspire the unwary visitor.

Sutherland notes that Jane Austen and her family were avid novel readers with wide-ranging and eclectic taste, ranging from classical literature to pulp fiction. She was "no snob". Sutherland is right about this: the cross-over quality of Austen's taste can also be seen in her theatre-going: she nearly always expressed a preference for the farce, which came after the main play. She was also a fan of the "illegitimate" theatres, which were forbidden to perform "licensed plays" (such as Shakespeare). As a writer interested in social class, Austen especially enjoyed after-pieces contrasting "high life" and "low" – farces such as *The Devil To Pay* and *High Life Below Stairs*, in which characters unexpectedly find themselves transformed into another social class – with hilarious consequences.

Sutherland also produced a handsome facsimile edition of the three notebooks of the young Austen (two of them now in the British Library, the other in the Bodleian), subtitled *In Her Own Hand*. It reproduces not just the manuscripts but also the size and format of the original. Sutherland is insightful on material culture, the physicality of the originals: they were shop-bought, stationer's notebooks, the covers are worn, suggesting frequent

usage and sustained re-reading. They show how the young Austen was keen to professionalize herself, providing her "works" with contents lists, dividing even short pieces into chapters, and inscribing dedications to people from "the humble author".

Sutherland argues that all three juvenile notebooks are "confidential publications", that is, "semi-public manuscripts . . . intended and crafted for circulation among family and friends". Insights are given into the collaborative nature of the Austen writing household. Jane collaborated with her sister Cassandra on a parody of Goldsmith's *History of England*. She also encouraged her niece Anna and nephew James Edward in their literary endeavours, and they both provided "continuations" to stories in *Volume the Third*. Anna co-wrote a play with her aunt, *Sir Charles Grandison*. Sutherland presents new evidence that James Edward rather than Austen herself was responsible for late emendations to "Kitty or the Bower".

These editions of Austen's youthful writings allow us to reassess their significance for her development as a writer. The best of the three volumes is universally agreed to be Volume the Second, begun when she was fifteen

ABOVE
Chloë Sevigny and Kate Beckinsale in *Love and Friendship* (2016), adapted from Austen's *Lady Susan* and directed by Whit Stillman

and containing the funniest parodies. The highlight is "Love and Freindship", a delightful, almost perfect, satire of the novel of sensibility. Its mockery of the clichés of the sentimental novel is executed with ruthless brilliance. The two heroines, Laura and Sophia, lie, cheat and steal – all in the name of sensibility. Whenever their bad behaviour is brought to account, they deflect admonishment by being overcome with excessive feeling.

Sutherland argues with great conviction that "Love and Freindship" is also a parody of the conduct-book genre, exemplified by Hester Chapone's Letters on the Improvement of the Mind, *Addressed to a Young Lady* (1773): "It is as if the young Jane Austen has strategically animated and empowered a whole regiment of teenage girls to openly revolt, in their anti-social and extravagant behaviour, against the conduct-book models of the schoolroom and the drawing room". In this world, the self-serving, manipulative, social-climbing heroines are the winners, and "good girls" are "merely an object of contempt".

Re-reading the youthful writings, one is struck again and again by the violence. A group of characters threaten murder by dagger, which shall be "steeped in your hearts blood". A sister poisons another sister and is "speedily raised to the gallows" for her perfidy. A child bites off her mother's fingers. There is also notable violence against the self. One young heroine inadvertently enters into an engagement with two gentlemen in the space of a single evening and kills herself by plunging into the river. Another is addicted "to the bottle", and drinks herself half to death. In "Love and Freindship", the two heroines, indulging in a bout of sensibility, are momentarily distracted by a road accident. They see "Two Gentlemen most elegantly attired but weltering in their blood". When the heroines discover that the gentlemen are in fact their husbands, they respond like characters in a sentimental novel: "Sophia shrieked and fainted on the Ground – I ran instantly mad". Sophia faints for so long that she catches cold, develops a fever and dies. Her final advice is not to faint but to run mad: "Beware of swoons, dear Laura . . . . A frenzy fit is not one quarter so pernicious; it is an exercise to the Body and if not too violent, is I dare say conducive to Health in its consequence".

Critics have long seen "Love and Freindship" as an embryo version of *Sense and Sensibility*. Both works, of course, are attacks on the novel of sensibility. Austen's first published novel establishes the type of novelist she

> *A sister poisons another sister and is 'speedily raised to the gallows' for her perfidy*

PAULA BYRNE

is not. Marianne's sensibility – her passion for dead leaves, her love of poetry and the picturesque – is mocked, as is her need to behave like a character in a sentimental novel: "Marianne would have thought herself very inexcusable had she been able to sleep at all the first night after parting from Willoughby. She would have been ashamed to look her family in the face the next morning, had she not risen from her bed more in need of repose than when she lay down on it". She spends whole days at the pianoforte "alternately singing and crying". We are not far from the anarchic world of "Love and Freindship". But Marianne is no cipher. Nor is she a hypocrite. The false delicacy of Lucy Steele, shedding phony tears of sensibility, is enough to remind us that Marianne's sensibility is genuine.

In "Love and Freindship", Laura's descent into madness, brought on by the death of her lover, is reminiscent of Ophelia, and is wickedly funny: "Talk not to me of Phaetons – Give me a violin. – I'll play to him and soothe him in his melancholy Hours – Look at that Grove of Firs – I see a Leg of Mutton – They told me Edward was not Dead;– But they deceived me – they took him for a cucumber". Marianne's breakdown, by contrast, is conveyed with almost clinical realism. It is characterized by uncontrollable crying ("tears streamed from her eyes with passionate violence"), refusal to eat, refusal to be consoled. She wants "at once solitude and continual change of pace". Her complexion takes on "a death-like paleness". Stretched on the bed, "choked by grief", she almost "screamed in agony . . . shocking as it was to witness". At her worst, her "nerves" can't even stand a rap on the door. She is brought close to death by her grief. On her recovery, she has been lobotomized into a new "calmness of

spirit", but still she dissolves into tears.

Early on, even when she is at her happiest and basking in her love affair with Willoughby, she is described as "not often really merry". Elinor's frustration with Marianne's ennui and indulgence in emotion, and disregard for the feelings of others, shows a misunderstanding of her sister's essential character. The more Elinor chides, the less Marianne listens. The more she begs her to "exert" herself, the more listless Marianne feels. The language employed to describe Marianne's mental breakdown is suffused with extremity: "violent sorrow", "violent oppression of spirits", "violence of affliction".

If Marianne were a young woman visiting her doctor today, she would tick a lot of boxes: insomnia, eating disorder, involuntary crying, pathological emotionality. She would be diagnosed as clinically depressed and perhaps even put on the list as a suicide risk. She might also be advised against reading Romantic poetry, rather as that wise physician of the emotions Anne Elliot advises another lovesick depressive, Captain Benwick, in *Persuasion*. He obsessively recites poetry "which imaged a broken heart, or a mind destroyed by wretchedness", leading Anne to say that "she thought it was the misfortune of poetry to be seldom safely enjoyed by those who enjoyed it completely; and that the strong feelings which alone could estimate it truly were the very feelings which ought to taste it but sparingly". She recommends Benwick to include a "larger allowance of prose in his daily study". Rather as a diet of P. G. Wodehouse is the best antidote to the flu, for anyone languishing with a broken heart there is no better tonic than the comedy – and indeed the cathartic violence – of Jane Austen's youthful writings. ∎

The sea, the sea

An Austen aficionado of the 1920s welcomes the first full publication of an unfinished work

AUTHOR: **ARTHUR McDOWALL**

This fragment of twelve chapters, which can be read in full now for the first time, is the one that has long intrigued us in quotations the end of the *Memoir of Jane Austen*. It has the peculiar interest of being the last work she attempted, for it was written at Chawton in the beginning of 1817, before that journey to Winchester from which she never returned. And as presented in this slim little volume – evidently by the skilled hand that produced the Oxford edition of the novelist – it brings us particularly close to her in the act of writing; the text, with all its roughnesses, has been printed just as she left it, and notes at the end show the corrections which she made *currente calamo*.

What strikes us in these pages from the very first is their unlikeness to the rest of her novels. It is not because her idiosyncrasy is lacking, as in *The Watsons*; yet there is a difference. Nothing could be less like her usual openings than to produce, after a carriage accident in a country lane, a lady and gentleman who remain anonymous for eleven pages. When Mr Parker declares his name and business,

and utters a paean – as lively as a speech out of Dickens – on the merits of Sanditon as an ideal spot for visitors, we begin to see why Jane Austen's relatives christened the fragment by that name and we forecast the novelty of the setting. Instead of collecting three or four families in a village she is going to put them in a "young and rising bathing-place".

The sheer fun of the thing is quite as distinctive. Jane Austen has thrown herself into the spirit of the place with a verve that seems positively riotous beside her usual demureness. She has

BELOW
"A calm" by James Gillray, 1810

time, all the same, to sketch in one or two characters who would ballast the story. Charlotte Heywood has the promise of a sensible, charming heroine; Lady Denham, the wealthy widow who is Mr Parker's rival as a promoter of Sanditon, has a genial downrightness and yet a twist of closeness that are sure to be dominating. There is the lovely Clara Brereton and just a glimpse of Mr Sidney Parker, who would have been one of the accomplished, moneyed young men of her fiction. But with Sir Edward Denham (Lady Denham's nephew), an infatuated young sentimentalist with the ambitions of a Lovelace, there begins a feast of absurdity. His mania for passionate novels is proclaimed with an almost burlesque exuberance which recalls some touches in *Northanger Abbey*, though it outdoes them.

It is with the other Parker relatives, however – three superlative hypochondriacs – that the fountain of merriment shoots highest. They are first pictured in a letter where Miss Diana, after an unusually severe attack of "spasmodic bile", declares that

she cannot come to Sanditon (of course, she does come):

I greive to say that I dare not attempt it, but my feelings tell me too plainly that in my present state, the Sea air wd. probably be the death of me. – And neither of my dear Companions will leave me, or I wd. promote their going down to you for a fortnight. But in truth, I doubt whether Susan's nerves wd. be equal to the effort. She has been suffering much from the Headache and Six Leaches a day for 10 days together relieved her so little that we thought it right to change our measures – and being convinced that much of the Evil lay in her Gum, I persuaded her to attack the disorder there. She has accordingly had 3 Teeth drawn, & is decidedly better, but

Austen has thrown herself into the spirit of the place with a verve that seems positively riotous

ARTHUR McDOWALL

her Nerves are a good deal deranged. She can only speak in a whisper – and fainted away twice this morning on poor Arthur's trying to suppress a cough. He, I am happy to say, is tolerably well – tho' more languid than I like – & I fear for his Liver.

Sadly we leave aside the inimitable tea-party in which Arthur Parker manoeuvres cunningly with buttered toast and cocoa. "Certainly", thought Charlotte, "Mr Arthur P.'s enjoyments in Invalidism were very different from his sister's – by no means so spiritualized. – A good deal of Earthy Dross hung about him." The reader may be also trusted to find out how a rich West Indian family and a young ladies' seminary from Camberwell upset anticipations.

There are moments when one is almost inclined to treat the whole fragment as a joke, but that would be to refuse Jane Austen her right to diversity. What more natural than that she should have found a counterpoise in those last months of ebbing health by releasing her unconquerable gaiety and mirth more freely than she had ever done in a novel? It is a curious, significant

rebound from *Persuasion*. If her laughter abounds here more than her irony, there is no failure of perceptiveness; witness her vision of the more basic traits which unite the whole clan of the Parkers. She has already, indeed, so prepared her Sanditon that it might well have furnished a scene and motif for the whole story. But the way she writes is, after all, the most significant thing in the fragment; there is such an unwonted and dramatic immediacy in the quick dialogue, the revelations of character, even the outdoor touches. It is tempting to think she was feeling for a new method. But part of this immediacy and swiftness is almost certainly there because the fragment is only the first, free draft of her story – an impression which is supported by the editor's view of her corrections. It would be absurd to judge what we have as we should judge a whole novel. But we may rejoice that it was written and has been released to delight us. Perhaps nothing in Jane Austen's fiction brings us nearer to the gaiety that sparkled in her life and is vivid still in her letters. ∎

The Life

Keeping it in the family

Writing about Jane Austen's life was, for a long time, in the hands of her family – a family who disagreed about what to do with their precious store of the author's papers

AUTHOR: **KATHRYN SUTHERLAND**

Jane Austen's chief heir and executor was her sister, Cassandra. In view of the periodic revival of interest in portraits of Jane Austen, it is worth looking again at the fortunes of two of Cassandra's own legacies. The better-known is the slight watercolour sketch she made of her sister in about 1810, now in the National Portrait Gallery. After family consultation, Jane's nephew James Edward Austen-Leigh commissioned a professional artist, James Andrews of Maidenhead, to execute a portrait from the sketch, and this provided the model for a steel engraving used as frontispiece to Austen-Leigh's *Memoir of Jane Austen* in 1870. It was the first public portrait of his aunt.

The difference between the engraving and Cassandra's original is evident to the most cursory glance. Her crude likeness is sharp-featured, pursed-lipped, unsmiling and withdrawn; in its Victorian refashioning, the face is softer, its expression pliant, and the eyes only pensively averted. At the time of the *Memoir*'s writing, Cassandra's sketch of Jane was the property of Cassy Esten,

their brother Charles's eldest daughter, and was considered by Anna Lefroy, James Edward's sister, to be "hideously unlike". Cassy Esten herself expressed relief at how the commissioned picture turned out: "I think the portrait is very much superior to any thing that could have been expected from the sketch it was taken from. It is a very pleasing, sweet face, tho', I confess to not thinking it much like the original; – but that, the public will not be able to detect". Caroline Austen, another sister of James Edward's, records something similar, telling her brother, "there is a look which I recognise as hers and though the general resemblance is not strong, yet as it represents a pleasant countenance it is so far a truth - & I am not dissatisfied with it".

As visual biographies the two tell quite different stories, whatever the claims of either might be to represent a human original. The Victorian image is quite appropriate to "St Aunt Jane of Steventon-cum-Chawton Canonicorum", as Austen-Leigh's hagiographic portrait was dubbed. His Jane is a comfortable figure, shunning fame and professional status, writing

PREVIOUS PAGES, ILLUSTRATION DAN NEATHER. THIS PAGE, REX FEATURES

RIGHT
Pencil and watercolour sketch of Jane Austen by her sister Cassandra, circa 1810

only in the intervals permitted from the more important domestic duties of a devoted daughter, sister and aunt. Yet Jane Austen herself remains a puzzle, with more than a hint of the Hampshire sphinx about her.

When, in 1926, Robert Chapman published his edition of Austen-Leigh's biography, the *TLS* (March 17, 1927) chiefly welcomed its reissue not for the life it recorded but for the manuscripts it described: "Here we may find . . . the last word about Jane Austen manuscripts, which not only is a thing to welcome for its own sake but may help to bring to light other manuscripts which are known to exist, or to have existed, but have been lost to sight". At that time, the discovery of an unknown manuscript novel, or at the very least some new fragments, did not seem impossible. In the 1920s, Chapman had published or was planning separate and handsome editions of the non-canonical writings that Austen-Leigh had chosen, after family consultation, to stretch out his biography (the cancelled chapter of *Persuasion*, *Lady Susan*, *The Watsons* and a synopsis of *Sanditon*), and he anticipated more manuscripts

coming to light as materials in family ownership now began to appear in the auction rooms.

Crucial to Chapman's ambitions in 1926 was the influence of later generations of the family as biographers and keepers of the archive. It is worth remembering how recently Jane Austen remained a family property, and particularly the property of the Austen-Leighs, that branch of the family descended from her eldest brother, James. In 1913, James Edward's grandson Richard Arthur Austen-Leigh had published with his uncle William Austen-Leigh an expanded biography, *Jane Austen: Her Life and Letters. A Family Record*, enlarging the 1870 account with materials drawn from other branches of the family. (Substantially rewritten under family commission by Deirdre Le Faye, *A Family Record* was reissued in 1989, bearing within it palimpsestically Austen-Leigh's *Memoir* and the 1913 Austen-Leighs' *Life and Letters*, and it stands as the acknowledged reference or "factual" biography.) The absence of biographical speculation from Chapman's edition of the earlier Austen-Leigh memoir registers a reluctance to engage critically with what in 1926 was still family business – a prudent act by a scholar and publisher eager to claim those literary remains still in family hands for his own shaping. Since then, though, things have changed. Virginia Woolf noted "how (Austen's) genius compelled her to absent herself", and by some curious process of compensation, the absence of a life to record has spawned a biographical industry.

"How many lives of Jane Austen do we need?" asked Richard Cohen in the *Daily Telegraph* on September 20, 1997, gesturing to the three titles newly or about-to-be published – by Valerie Grosvenor Myer, David Nokes and Claire

Tomalin. Cohen was not aware of a fourth, as yet a gleam in Carol Shields's eye; but four biographies in as many years is no bad record for an author about whom there is so little to know. And that little we do know has been determined, more than with any other famous individual, by family. The records are the product of particular family views, against which might be set other, different family recollections. Surviving letters, manuscripts and other material witnesses remained largely in family hands for the 100 years after Jane Austen's death. There is no non-fictional evidence for a "self" other than that constructed within the bounds of family. No diaries have come down to suggest the existence of an inner life, a self apart. The modern biographer, for whom the interest of a literary life generally increases in proportion to its inwardness, is defeated by this absence of a resistant private voice.

If there is no autobiographical record, there is also very little by way of a non-familial social or public record. The archive of Jane Austen's publisher, the famously sociable John Murray, has yielded nothing but the barest details of a professional relationship – no hints of literary parties at which Miss Austen might have been a guest. The opportunistic Henry Austen, in his brief 1833 "Memoir" – a formal fashioning of a proper lady novelist by a brother who had refashioned himself on more than one occasion – can only mention as noteworthy an event in her life which did not take place: a meeting with the glamorous French novelist Germaine de Staël, proposed for 1814.

The decision to prepare a biography was taken by James Edward Austen-Leigh in the late 1860s, and he wrote in a spirit of censorship as well as communication. His authority as memorialist was unquestionable – the only son of Jane's eldest brother, James,

LEFT
Engraving of Jane and Cassandra doing needlework

BELOW
Mr and Mrs Austen

he had as a boy of nineteen attended her body to the grave. Admiral Sir Francis Austen, her last surviving sibling, had died in August 1865, aged ninety-one. His death marked the end of her generation and therefore a moment for gathering the family record in written form. In addition, those nieces and nephews who had known her when they were children were also now old and wished to hand on, within the family at least, some account of their distinguished relation. The anxiety attending the composition of the *Memoir* is evident in the files of family correspondence in the Austen-Leigh Archive (Hampshire Record Office) and the National Portrait Gallery. Significantly, in the 1860s, the public interest in Jane Austen's novels, mounting gradually since the 1830s, provided cause for concern. There was the fear that a non-family-derived biography might be attempted and, more worrying, that a younger branch of the family might exploit unpublished materials and make public something injudicious.

Austen-Leigh's cousin, the hack novelist Catherine Hubback, had already cashed in on her aunt's famous name, and seemed poised to do so again. Her novel *The Younger Sister* (1850), with a dedication to Aunt Jane, was based quite closely on the Austen fragment *The Watsons*. The anxiety in the 1860s was that, with several more novels to her credit, Hubback might have her sights set on the fragment known in the family as *Sanditon*. Austen-Leigh's sister Anna Lefroy, then the legal owner of the Sanditon manuscript, was suspicious, writing to her brother on August 8, 1862: "The Copy (of Sanditon) which was taken, not given, is now at the mercy of Mrs. Hubback, & she will be pretty sure to make use of it as soon as she thinks she safely may". Austen-Leigh's grander

cousins the Knatchbulls, descendants of Jane's niece Fanny Knight, had their own collection of Austen manuscripts and memorabilia; but Fanny was now senile and other family members were unable or reluctant to find them when Austen-Leigh came asking for help.

Their different portrait of a socially improved and passionate Aunt Jane would be made public by Fanny's son Lord Brabourne in 1884, in *Letters of Jane Austen*. For the Austen-Leigh account, his two sisters, Anna Lefroy and Caroline Austen, supplied intimate memories. Anna, James Edward and Caroline had inhabited her birthplace at Steventon, after their father, James, took over as curate there on the retirement to Bath of his father, George Austen. All three were closer to Jane's Hampshire roots (socially as well as geographically) than other branches of the family. Anna's memories reached back farthest, to Steventon days, when Jane Austen was barely twenty, and they are touchingly quirky. For her, then a child of three or four, aunts came in pairs, Cassandra and Jane mysteriously distinguishable only by a now forgotten detail of their bonnets. Caroline remembered the daily routine later at Chawton – Aunt Jane's early morning piano playing and stories about fairyland, invented to delight her little nieces, in which the fairies "had all characters of their own".

If there is a common thread other

That little we know has been determined, more than with any other famous individual, by her

KATHRYN SUTHERLAND

than personal memory, it is Cassandra, who was almost solely responsible for the preservation (or destruction), and subsequent distribution among brothers, nieces and nephews, of letters, manuscripts and mementoes. She decisively shaped, through stewardship of the archive and through conversation, what was available (and to whom) in the next generation. One of the mysteries the cousins unravel as they collect and compare their portions of knowledge is exactly what each has been given to know. As Caroline Austen put it in a letter to her brother: "I am sure you will do justice to what there is but I feel it must be a difficult task to dig up the materials, so carefully have they been buried out of our sight by the past generat-(ion)". Anna speculates: "There may be other sources of information, if we could get at them – Letters may have been preserved", but she does not know this with any certainty. A few years later she concludes:

The occasional correspondence between the Sisters when apart from each other would as a matter of course be destroyed by the Survivor – I can fancy what the indignation of Aunt Cassa would have been at the mere idea of its' being read and commented upon by any of us, nephews and nieces, little or great – and indeed I I [sic] think myself she was right, in that as in most other things.

The collected letters of Jane Austen, as they are now available to us, only came together in 1932, and so the reconnection of the various parts of the epistolary archive considerably post-dates both the *Memoir* and the publication of the largest Knatchbull cache in 1884. We simply do not know the extent of Cassandra's careful work of destruction and whether this accounts for the unyielding nature of the evidence – for the difficulty we have in recovering anything more satisfactory

JANE AUSTEN'S HOUSE MUSEUM

than a partial and unconfiding life of Jane Austen. Lord Brabourne's description of the letters he edited as the "confidential outpourings" of one soul to another is from the evidence wildly inaccurate, but perfectly explicable in terms of family rivalry - his claim to market another Jane Austen.

What we do know is that her nieces and nephew did not tell the whole truth about Jane Austen and her family as they knew it. Writing to her brother with memories and stories from the past, Caroline makes a distinction between what she has to tell and what she gives for him to print: "I should not mind telling any body, at this distance of time - but printing and publishing seem to me very different from talking about the past"; and "this is not a fact to be written and printed but you have authority for saying she did mind it". The stories she sketches, got from Aunt

ABOVE
A letter from Austen to Cassandra, March 2 1814, in which she describes her brother Henry's reaction to *Mansfield Park*

Cassandra and from her mother, Mary Lloyd, refer respectively to Jane's marriage proposal from Harris Bigg-Wither in December 1802 and the Revd George Austen's decision late in 1800 to leave Steventon and move to Bath. The existence of a second brother, the handicapped but long-lived George Austen, is concealed, and Edward, the third brother, is presented as the second. There is no reference to the jailing of Jane's aunt Mrs Leigh Perrot on a charge of shoplifting in Bath.

Neither piece of discretion is surprising; both are matters of honour and good taste. Austen-Leigh was his great-uncle Leigh Perrot's heir, adding Leigh to his name on his great-aunt's death in 1837. But the publicity of the imprisonment and trial, occurring only a year before the Austens moved to Bath, must have continued to hang in the air of such a gossip-driven city and to affect the family's social standing. For this reason, we long to know more of Jane Austen's impressions of life there.

Another sketch accepted in the family as of Aunt Jane, and also in Cassy Esten's portion of the inheritance, was in Anna Lefroy's possession by 1869, when she described it in a letter to her brother as bearing "a good deal of resemblance". Earlier, in 1862, she had written of it, "I would give a good deal, that is as much as I could afford, for a sketch which Aunt Cassandra made of her in one of their expeditions - sitting down out of doors, on a hot day, with her bonnet strings untied". Dated 1804, it was used as a frontispiece to Chapman's 1932 edition of the *Letters*, and on the front cover of *A Portrait of Jane Austen* by Lord David Cecil (1978). In a letter to the *TLS* (October 11, 1941), Chapman went so far as to assert "that it is, in all probability, almost all we have". It seems fitting that the portrait both Anna and Chapman endorse as having the strongest claim is a back view only. ∎

Emma

volume 3, chapter 6

**It was a sweet view – sweet to the eye and the mind.
English verdure, English culture, English comfort,
seen under a sun bright, without being oppressive.**

A perfect novel about a supposedly perfect heroine,
Emma appeared early in 1816: its match-making protagonist
interferes ridiculously in others' love lives, but, in a sense, very little happens.
The genius of Jane Austen comes through here in the way she
needs none of the sensational elements on which lesser novelists depend.

ILLUSTRATION: **DARREN SMITH**

THE LIFE

Plainly Jane

Controversy has long surrounded the image of Jane Austen, as enigmatically
fixed by her sister Cassandra, and long sought after by later
generations of biographers and admirers

As Kathryn Sutherland mentions in the preceding essay, authenticated portraits of Jane Austen are scarce – and the watercolour sketch of her by Cassandra Austen reproduced on page 57 has become, in adapted form, an overfamiliar sight. It forms the basis of the Austen portrait to be seen on the new £10 banknote, for instance.

Cassandra also produced a sketch of her sister facing away from her (1), "sitting down out of door on a hot day", as Austen's niece Anna Lefroy later put it, "with her bonnet strings untied". It is tempting to see an elusive quality in this "portrait" that is appropriate to the author; but this hasn't stopped people making intriguing claims to see Austen's likeness elsewhere. When the Prince Regent's librarian, James Stanier Clarke, invited her to Carlton House in London, did he produce an elegant image (2) of an author his master admired so much? Did the artist Ozias Humphry, many years earlier, execute a sketch of Austen as a girl armed with a parasol (3)? Could Austen's biographer Paula Byrne be right that there is indeed a portrait of the author at work, crowned with laurels and sharing her desk space with a cat (4)?

FROM LEFT
1. Cassandra's "portrait" of Austen facing away from the viewer
2. The Stanier Clarke portrait
3. The Rice portrait
4. The Byrne portrait
5. The Jane Austen Centre waxwork
6. Adam Roud's sculpture

Controversy surrounds such claims – but there are modern alternatives. The Jane Austen Centre in Bath unveiled a waxwork (5) in 2014 that is claimed to be the nearest "anyone has come to the real Jane Austen for 200 years"; and, for Austen's bicentenary, the sculptor Adam Roud has produced a bronze (6) intended to adorn the Hampshire town of Basingstoke, not far from Steventon, where Austen grew up. It is said to be the first sculpture of Jane Austen – perhaps it shows her on her way to meet Cassandra on one of those hot days so suitable for sitting around and sketching. ∎

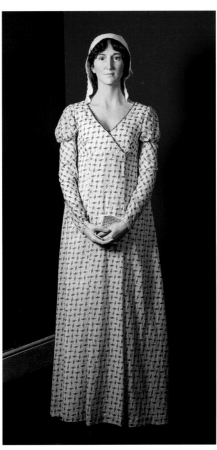

THE LIFE

Niece work

A bleak and beautiful reimagining of Austen's life on film

AUTHOR: **KATHRYN SUTHERLAND**

This latest contribution to the indefatigable Jane Austen film industry grows from one of the few attested events in Austen's life, which – though well-known to Janeites – is likely to cast her in a fresh light with a wider audience. The scene is Manydown Park, Hampshire, home of the Austen family's close friends, the Bigg-Withers, where on the evening of Thursday December 2, 1802, Jane Austen, just short of her twenty-seventh birthday, received a proposal of marriage from the young heir to the estate. This may not have been her only offer, but it is the only one we know for certain that she accepted. Overnight she changed her mind. "Tell me I have done the right thing. Tell me I was right to change my mind" – Jane's plea to her sister Cassandra as spoken in Gwyneth Hughes's script for *Miss Austen Regrets* becomes the mainspring of the story that follows.

Fast-forward twelve years and Jane Austen is a successful author, with three published novels to her credit, including the fashionable hit *Pride and Prejudice*. She attends the wedding of her niece and namesake Jane Anna Austen to Ben Lefroy, relative of Tom Lefroy, with whom she had flirted and possibly been in love almost twenty years before (and who was the male interest in the 2007 biopic *Becoming Jane*). Another niece, Fanny Knight, asks her aunt to vet various young men as potential husbands. She renews her acquaintance with a clergyman, Brook (Edward) Bridges, whose romantic attentions almost ten years before she had failed to encourage. A pattern begins to emerge: novels that uphold the social importance of marriage and its economic urgency for women; an aunt who affectionately and intensively counsels her nieces on their love lives; and a woman who has flouted

these norms to cultivate fastidiousness in her own life. "I simply went off the whole idea of marrying anybody", she remarks to Bridges.

As she approaches forty, Jane Austen reviews her own past choices in those of her nieces. At the same time, the potential for regret is brought into sharper focus by looming financial crisis: the collapse of her brother Henry's bank and the lawsuit threatening her brother Edward's Hampshire estate, which includes the cottage she shares with her mother and sister. It is in light of these events that old Mrs Austen (Phyllida Law) directs at her daughter a recrimination that might come straight from one of her own novels: to be rich is to be safe. If Jane had married Harris Bigg, her mother and sister would now be secure.

From slight but suggestive evidence, Gwyneth Hughes, an acclaimed crime dramatist, has crafted a thrifty and compelling script. How might Austen's life appear if we view it from her decision to renege on a promise to marry? What are we to make of the inclusion in her two late novels, *Emma* and *Persuasion*, of a woman who

marries in middle age and another whose broken engagement eight years before has left her in an emotional wasteland? By drawing heavily and skilfully on Jane Austen's letters to Cassandra and to Fanny Knight, stitching in and reapportioning to these later years social and personal observations and insights from much earlier correspondence, Hughes has broken new ground. Austen's letters have received little serious critical attention, yet they fizz with wit and malice. Fragments of social and psychic

To be rich is to be safe. If Jane had married Harris Bigg, her mother and sister would now be safe

KATHRYN SUTHERLAND

drama, they find in Hughes's screenplay a voice whose authenticity and modernity will take many by surprise.

Played with great assurance by Olivia Williams, this is a complicated, controversially adult Jane Austen: tart and barbed, amusing, desperately flirtatious, lonely, by turns intolerant, dependent and afraid. Imogen Poots is appealing as Fanny. In this absorbing drama of only ninety minutes, few other characters are as finely realized. Hugh Bonneville is sufficiently sympathetic as Austen's rejected suitor and confidant Brook Bridges to suggest that she might have combined marriage with novel writing; Greta Scacchi injects a credible impatience into her intense portrayal of Cassandra Austen.

Miss Austen Regrets is a bleak and a beautiful film which derives its eloquence from the intelligent complicity between Hughes's screenplay, Jeremy Lovering's direction and Williams's taut performance. Its representation of Williams as another

ABOVE
Olivia Williams as Jane Austen, Greta Scacchi as Cassandra and Imogen Poots as Fanny Knight

camera eye is innovative, a visual equivalent to the nice discriminations of Austen's critical writing style. We are constrained within the orbit of her perception – literally at times within her body. We share a sensory and a critical kinship with her. The effect reaches a disturbing climax in the triangulation of Austen, Fanny and the young physician Charles Haden (Jack Huston) towards the end of the film.

Lovering's direction has found a new style, more observational and less encumbered than either the heritage-heavy sets of the 1990s or the muddy-hem sprightliness of recent adaptations. Detail is alternately drab, like Austen's frugally recycled wardrobe, or luminous. This extends to the domestic particulars of the Austen women's lives at Chawton, where objects, bathed in light and seen through doorways or framed in windows, are discovered in shape, colour and texture as simply themselves, the "little matters" of Jane Austen's life and letters. ∎

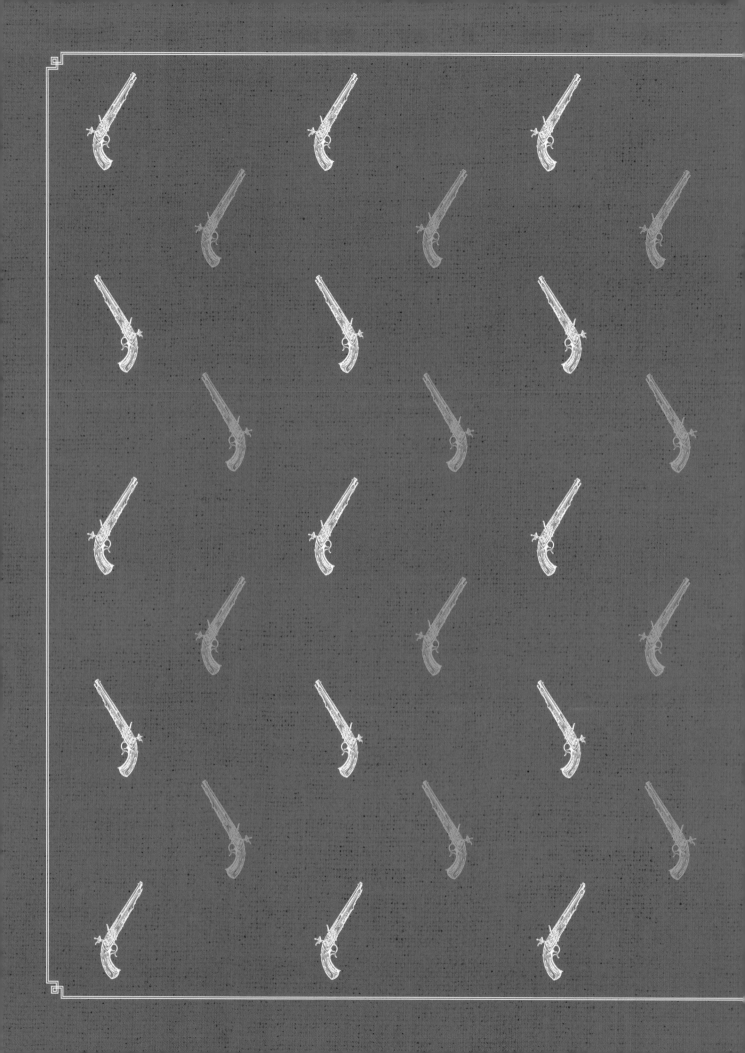

The Times

THE TIMES

Sex and the Georgian city

Living in London – which the Austen family knew as both residents and visitors, and where Jane Austen's publishers were based – in a time of architectural distinction and hidden vice

AUTHOR: **STELLA TILLYARD**

In the eighteenth century, foreign visitors to England were quick to sense a relationship between architecture, the home and the national character. The English "prefer the most miserable cottage hired in their own name, to more convenient apartments in another house", wrote the German observer Von Archenholz in 1791, as quoted by Amanda Vickery in *Behind Closed Doors*. He was not the only one to make this connection between space, architecture, home, goods and identity.

In 1780, the redoubtable Dowager Countess of Home, stepping out of her magnificent town house in Portman Square (constructed by James Wyatt in 1772 and sumptuously remodelled by Robert Adam three years later) walked into a neighbourhood that was home to thousands of prostitutes. The finest of London's town houses, in St James's Square, were only yards from King's Place, a street that housed dozens of London's most expensive prostitutes. In the capital, in the very crucible of modernity, where architecture conferred status, and goods made people who they were, there was no more lucrative chattel than female flesh. London in the eighteenth century had more prostitutes per capita than any other European city. What impact, if any, did the use of prostitutes by husbands, sons, servants and visitors have on the notion of selfhood as inherent in the private and the domestic? How did what people saw or bought on the streets or in bagnios affect what they thought and how they lived within their homes? Was home the more sweet and to be cherished because so many did not have one? Was the sense of self that Vickery writes about, created from what she calls "the universe of possessions", as much defensive as constructive; a shutting out as much as a building within? Might not being "at home" make sense then, and now, if set against what was outside and at variance with the ideas of household and matrimony?

Rachel Stewart, in *The Town House in Georgian London*, has a sober sense that the town house gained meaning and attraction from its opposite, the country seat. In the period she considers, roughly between the

RIGHT
Benjamin Smith, "Street Walkers'" (1786); a fashionably dressed man encountering a courtesan

accession of George III in 1760 and the beginning of the long conflict with France after the French Revolution, the town house reached the height of its architectural spread and expression, but it also became the site of longing and opprobrium in equal measure. Stewart's straightforward and thorough examination of the cultural and architectural history of the town house offers a clear account of a distinctive element of London's built environment, and it also shows that for a small, influential body of people, the development of the town house led to a loosening of bonds with the countryside, with ancestry and dynastic duty, and a new idea of the self as urban, singular and perhaps even modern.

The Great Fire saw a shift of domestic architecture away from the City of London in the late seventeenth century; meanwhile the waning power of the Court and the rise in the importance of Parliament and professional politics meant that increasing numbers of aristocrats established town houses in London's West End. Building spread northwards

STREET WALKERS

Publish'd April 28 1786 by S. W. Fores Nº 3 Piccadilly, Battle Bad.

from the streets around St James's Palace in the first decades of the eighteenth century, and by the end of the Seven Years War in 1763, the "rage of building" led to extensive development west and north of Cavendish Square (begun 1717) in Marylebone, particularly in Portman Square and in the grid of streets bounded by Oxford Street, the New (now Euston) Road to the north and Portland Place to the east. At the same time, the Bedford Estate was filling in the squares and streets of Bloomsbury, and other isolated developments, such as the Adelphi, south of the Strand, were attracting fashionable tenants. Much of the land was owned by aristocratic families and therefore entailed, or it was in the hands of corporate landowners who developed it to provide a long-term steady income. As a result most houses were held on leases and building was large-scale and uniform.

Despite the development of the "palace front", which pulled a row of three-bay houses into a single design reminiscent of a grander building, both the basic layout and the external appearance of the town house remained remarkably consistent throughout the eighteenth century. There were occasional grand, "stand alone" commissions within the architecture of particular squares, Berkeley Square or St James's Square, for instance, and interesting experiments with form such as Robert Taylor's Palladian-windowed house in Soho Square; but the majority of houses had two or three "good" rooms facing the street and a number of smaller rooms at the back, basement kitchens and small gardens or mews behind. Perhaps in part because of this uniformity, great attention was paid to remodelling and fitting up houses; the Adam brothers in particular provided ingenious, elegant and often expensive solutions to the problems of small sites

and standard floor plans, with apses and ceilings, wall reliefs and chimney pieces creating integrated neo-classical interiors that made the most of light and space.

The transitory nature of the town house, its leasehold status and its interchangeability made it the site of dreams and consumption. Stewart points out that a town house was usually described as belonging to somebody, whereas, in the country, a man and his family were described as pertaining to a particular house or estate. In London people would use their property to define them as they wished. Some of the best town houses were commissioned by widows who had little status in the dynastic realm of the countryside, where they would be relegated to the dower house. In town, they could visit, entertain and feel themselves on an equal footing with

ABOVE
View of St James's Square from the south-east corner, London, 1812

their neighbours, and they could spend their money on furnishings and decorative schemes. Not surprisingly, many soon stayed in their much-loved town houses all the year round.

By the end of the century the notion of the town house was weakening; aristocratic younger sons, bachelors, spinsters, widows and officers' wives began to live in town permanently. In 1809, when her husband went out to Portugal to command the British Army, Kitty, Lady Wellington, arrived in London and rented Number 11 Harley Street. She had no house in the country, and neither did her next-door neighbour, Sir William Beechey. The Dowager Duchess of Leinster lived at Number 14 and left town only occasionally for a modest cottage in Wimbledon. For professionals and aristocrats such as these London became, sometimes briefly, often

reckoned there were 62,000, and the police magistrate Patrick Colquhoun calculated in 1795 that London had 50,000 prostitutes, about half of whom sold themselves only occasionally. Were prostitutes so ubiquitous in London that they were unremarkable? If there were 25,000 prostitutes in London, say, how many clients might they have had from a male population of about 350,000? However you calculate it, the answer is a great many.

Was the Georgian home, then, a place of double lives, from which respectable men regularly nipped out for a quick something off the street? Did wives and mothers know and care little? Did the Evangelical revival of the last quarter of the century usher in not just an era of greater restraint and concern but a widespread change in sexual attitudes too; or did everything simply shift geographically and go underground? We know a good deal about attitudes to and the practice of adultery in the eighteenth century, but relatively little about the purchase of sex on a large scale.

If the 3,000 figure is nearer the mark, and was reflected on a smaller scale in provincial cities and towns, then the spinsters and wives of Amanda Vickery's book could go about the business of running their households undisturbed by the thought that thousands of women were out on the streets or running and living in bawdy houses and seraglios all around them. In her excellent chapter on bachelor households Vickery says that unmarried men in eighteenth-century England longed for matrimony and that, "far removed from twenty-first century fears that settling-down extinguishes virility, establishing a household was believed to give it full rein". If those larger figures on prostitution are even half-accurate, however, such a cheerful view of men at home needs to be rethought. ■

permanently, home. Over time the design of the town house, reduced to two bays and between five and two storeys, became the frustratingly cramped and distinctive style of London building that endured for the next hundred years.

The distinction between the town house and townhouse was anyway blurred, often depending more on who lived there than on any distinctive architectural feature. Many speculatively built three-bay houses were in multiple occupancy from the start, broken up into apartments or inhabited by a family who rented out rooms or whole floors. All around Soho Square, and throughout Marylebone by the mid-eighteenth century, actresses, prostitutes and courtesans lived in small apartments, side by side with aristocratic and professional leaseholders. Vice was an all-pervasive part of London life in the eighteenth century, and the profits of vice fuelled the building boom that Stewart describes.

Modern assessments of the numbers of prostitutes in the mid-eighteenth century, based on admissions to the Magdalen House and the Lock Hospital, suggest a figure of 3,000 common prostitutes at any time, a number that does not include courtesans or kept women. In 1758, however, one writer

Vice was an all-pervasive part of London life in the eighteenth century

STELLA TILLYARD

THE TIMES

Wives and daughters

Recovering the records of women's lives in Georgian England

AUTHOR: **CLAIRE TOMALIN**

In the record offices of Lancashire, Yorkshire and Cumbria, the historian Amanda Vickery found a gold mine of women's history: letters and pocket-book diaries kept by the daughters, wives and mothers of gentlemen of the eighteenth and early nineteenth centuries, allowing us to hear their voices as they experience courtship, marriage, motherhood and widowing, and to enjoy direct accounts of their domestic and social preoccupations. Material of this kind is precious.

Certain characters burst out of the pages of Vickery's book *The Gentleman's Daughter* (1998) to dominate the narrative with the force of their personalities. One is Elizabeth Parker ("Parky" to her friends, 1726–81), a lesser landowner's daughter whose letters and diaries chart most of her life, starting with a seven-year wooing by a cousin of whom her father disapproved. Her lover tried every line of attack, urging her to clandestine night-time meetings, and won her in the end by the old ruse of telling her he was preparing to marry someone else. At this she persuaded her father to relent,

and they were married. But she was soon left a widow with small sons to bring up alone; and after another seven years she eloped – to Gretna Green – with a young man eighteen years her junior. This marriage was a disaster for both parties. She was dropped by her most important living male relative, her brother. There were no children, her husband came to resent and indeed hate her, and he took to drink.

Although Elizabeth struggled to keep her dignity, she sank in the social scale as he wasted their money, roistering in the kitchen with tenants and servants (sometimes it sounds almost like *Wuthering Heights*). Meanwhile, her brother improved his status, marrying a baronet's daughter. His son went into parliament; her sons became tradesmen.

All this is documented in Elizabeth's own hand, with records of her hiring and management of servants, her dinners and tea parties, her snobberies and wounded feelings, her second husband's blows and curses; as well as a surprising touch, her successful marketing of an anti-rabies medicine developed by her first husband, which

she sold all over the north of England at one shilling a bottle until her death. (It was presumably never put to the test on an actual case of rabies.)

Elizabeth's jolly cousin Bessy is another striking character. She lodged in London with her brother until she was nearly forty, when she married a fifty-year-old bachelor schoolmaster. The marriage was deeply satisfying to both, and they paraded their satisfaction in letters to relations, Bessy proclaiming she was "not ashamed of my passion" for her "lord and master". In spite of her age, there were four babies, and she breast-fed them all. In fact, little Betsy was shod before she was weaned, and "My Littel Boy has not for this three week been from my Bed or lap half hour at a time. For to my shame (Tho' happy it was for him) I still suckel him". This was in the 1760s, about the same time that Jane Austen's mother was weaning her infants briskly at two or three months and sending them to be reared in the village.

The decision to breast-feed or not seems to have been much more an individual choice than a matter of fashion. Bessy was by no means tied

down by her maternal and domestic duties; she went out as much as she pleased to enjoy the pleasures of London life, "frolicking" to the theatre or gawping at the royal family. And her good-humoured husband respected her taste for gadding: "came the Coach to the Door and away whisked Madam to the Assembly as usual".

Then there is the heiress Anne Wilmer, also from the middle of the eighteenth century, who condescended to give her hand to a rich mercer's son, William Gossip, manager of the York Assembly Rooms. He was clever and charming, and theirs was another demonstratively affectionate marriage. They hated to be separated and wrote to tell one another so, often invoking the marriage bed: "I wish I had my poor Dear in his own bed with me. I think you would be beter (sic)", etc. A rich and happy couple, they built a mansion on their large estate in Wharfedale, in addition to their solid town house in York, and William became a Justice of the Peace and Deputy Lieutenant for the West Riding. Only the fates of their eleven children were disappointing. Most died young, and the heir outraged them by marrying down, a secret match to the daughter of a poor Halifax mantua-maker. He was disinherited. One son studied medicine, others were apprenticed to hosiers or went into the Army.

The women figuring in these records were not aristocrats. They came from middle-class families, genteel, proper and prosperous for the most part; some married to landowners, some to professional men, some to tradesmen. And their children took divergent paths, as we have seen. One thing that emerges strongly from Vickery's account is the high degree of mobility of late Georgian life, as men and women moved themselves up or tumbled down the social snakes and ladders board. This

certainly tallies with observations of the Hampshire families which I made in my researches for the biography of Jane Austen.

What is very clear is just how individual and unpredictable each life and each family was, and how they refuse to conform to the generalizations of historians. Part of the purpose of Vickery's book is indeed to attack the theses of academic historians who have constructed a narrative of "decline and fall" in the status of Englishwomen, following some notional golden age in which they are said to have been powerful working members of society. This golden age has been variously set from the Middle Ages to the years immediately preceding the industrial revolution; but whether or whenever it was, there has been pretty general agreement that the nineteenth century was a nadir for women, in which their lives were "drained of economic purpose and public responsibility".

Vickery's thesis is that women in the Georgian period – which extended, of course, through the first third of the nineteenth century – were in truth more confident and more autonomous than is "usually allowed". She suggests further that the Victorian women who fought for the right to education, suffrage and professional training were seeking "to extend yet further the gains made by their Georgian predecessors". She supports this by claiming that Georgian women enjoyed responsibility and a significant amount of economic power in the domestic sphere; had considerable freedom in choosing their husbands; participated in the expanding social world of the assembly room, public gardens, music meetings and theatres; and in charitable and reforming groups such as the anti-slavery movement.

Whether these activities were really the forerunners of the feminist activities

BELOW Willoughby carrying Marianne after her accident; an illustration by C. E. Brock for *Sense and Sensibility*

of the nineteenth century is open to argument, to say the least. For one thing, the later nineteenth-century struggles were fired by bitterness against the status quo, and taken up by middle-class women who specifically felt they lacked autonomy over their lives. The bitterness certainly had its roots earlier. Leaving aside Mary Wollstonecraft and her circle, there is the experience of the Lancastrian Ellen Weeton (1776–?1844), whom Vickery actually includes in her book. For Weeton, there was little enough autonomy, shortage of money forcing her into governessing, and a tyrannical husband taking her child from her and reducing her to the point of starvation. Vickery concedes that Weeton suffered almost dehumanizing ill-treatment, but does not quote or even refer to her private writing about the situation of her sex. For instance, Weeton recalled as a child hearing her father express the wish that all his children should be boys, not because he did not love girls as well, but "unless a father can provide independent fortunes for his daughters, they must either be made mop squeezers, or mantua makers, whereas sons can easily make their way in the world". This thoughtful sea captain was killed young fighting the Americans, and his clever daughter had to become, not a mop squeezer it's true, but a governess; and when she married, her husband turned out to be a brute.

She expressed the view that the sexes were equal, and that society would be better organized were they treated equally. Thus, in 1809, she wrote to her lawyer brother:

Why are not females permitted to study physic, divinity, astronomy, &c., with their attendants, chemistry, botany, logic, mathematics, &c. To be sure the mere study is not prohibited, but the practise is in a great measure. Who would employ a female physician? who would listen to a female divine, except to ridicule? I could myself almost laugh at the idea.

The crucial point here is poverty. Weeton, like Wollstonecraft, was bred to be a lady, but then found herself thrown on a world which offered no decent alternative to marriage. Before them, Richardson had meditated (in *Sir Charles Grandison*) on the difficult situation of unsupported ladies, and whether Protestant nunneries might be a partial solution to their problems; an idea Sheridan also took up. But even rich and married ladies expressed their discontents at times. In the (unpublished) letters and diaries of Eliza Chute, the wife of a Hampshire MP at the end of the eighteenth century, there are clear expressions of dissatisfaction with the position of wives:

Mr Chute . . . seems to think it strange that I should absent myself from him for four & twenty hours when he is at home, tho' it appears in the natural order of things that he should quit me for business or pleasure, such is the difference between husbands & wives. The latter are sort of tame animals, whom the men always expect to find at home ready to receive them: the former are lords of the creation free to go where they please.

There are other cases that support Vickery's view, of course. Charlotte

The women figuring in these records were not aristocrats. They came from middle-class families

CLAIRE TOMALIN

Smith (1749–1806), married in her early teens to an uncongenial and errant husband who became bankrupt, displayed extraordinary energy and was able to maintain herself and her many children entirely by her pen, becoming a successful poet and novelist. Was she a model to nineteenth-century women writers? You think at once of a later Charlotte (Brontë, 1816–55), admonished by Robert Southey to give up the idea of becoming a writer and stick to her needle and domestic duties. Fanny Burney wrote for money and kept what she earned in the 1790s, when she was married; whereas William Gaskell, in the 1850s, pocketed his wife's earnings as the cheques arrived. And it was in 1848 that Geraldine Jewsbury wrote *The Half Sisters*, her impassioned attack on the way in which English ladies were infantilized by their upbringing. Mary Shelley, struggling to make a living by her pen, wrote, in 1843, that she abhorred and shrank from "a public life for women".

Vickery points to many ladies among her sample who felt satisfaction at their position in life, and it is true that a polite husband, a sufficient income, obedient servants and access to some company and amusements did appear to meet the needs of most who enjoyed these blessings. But it seems to me that one message that emerges from her book is the very great difficulty of making general statements about the

behaviour of genteel women or their view of their own position, either in the eighteenth or the nineteenth century. Consider that Jane Austen's paternal aunt Philadelphia, an orphan, travelled to India alone in the 1750s to get herself a husband, but a generation later Jane's careful parents did not dream of letting her travel across the southern counties of England without an escort. Does this represent a general shift in attitude, or was it rather that Mrs Austen decreed what her daughters might do from the traditions of the family in which she had grown up?

It seems likely that traditions running through the female line are responsible for many such features in the life of a family; but because they were not formalized or written down, but simply passed on verbally from mother to daughter, and taken for granted, it is impossible to be certain about them. So it is for childbirth practices, the feeding and weaning of babies, ideas about contraception and sex, all very poorly documented. Sets of family letters are precious in these areas, and Vickery's book is full of fine details and discoveries. In spite of some awkward terminology – "heterosociality", "the elite mistress" – we are given the feeling of life as it was lived by her ladies, as they express their status through furniture and china, make careful note of food prices, take pleasure in discussing new fashions, grumble about an ungrateful maid or an inconsiderate man who smokes over the table, or lets off his gun in the next room; or the joy of having a small daughter, "all over so fat and soft". Again and again, their words surprise and charm. The eighteenth was, of course, the great century of increasing female literacy, in which the women of England discovered they could not only enjoy reading novels and poems but write them, too. ∎

THE TIMES

These conflicted times

The age of Jane Austen was also an age of constant military activity –
and might even be seen as the first age of total war

AUTHOR: **SUDHIR HAZAREESINGH**

Societies implacably mobilized against each other, in conflicts ending only in unconditional surrender; large-scale conscript armies, whose titanic clashes provoke mass slaughter; the enemy utterly dehumanized, with executions of prisoners and unspeakable atrocities against civilians; territories precariously controlled by occupying armies, whose power and authority are systematically eroded by guerrilla groups; and war and military martyrdom represented as the highest of human endeavours.

Contrary to conventional wisdom, as David A. Bell suggested in *The First Total War* (2007), these features of modern war were not born in the World Wars of the twentieth century. Rather, their origin lies in the Revolutionary and Napoleonic conflicts of 1792–1815, which gave birth to what Carl Schmitt later described as the norm of "absolute enmity". In Bell's view, this was moment that – in addition to consecrating Europe's largest empire since the Middle Ages, and its greatest conqueror since Charlemagne – shaped the modern understanding and practice of "total" warfare, carrying it

across the murderous battlefields of the twentieth century.

This argument about the foundational nature of the Napoleonic Wars had been made before, notably in Jean-Yves Guiomar's *L'Invention de la guerre totale* (2004). Bell's rendering was much more radical. First, his argument rested on a bold vision of the transformation of the modern culture of war in eighteenth-century Europe. He contrasted the sedate, aristocratic conception of limited warfare, wonderfully symbolized by the 145 tons of baggage which accompanied the Duke of Cumberland into battle, with the frenzied, messianic and apocalyptic qualities of the French Revolutionary wars. In order to make his case, Bell also integrated approaches to the history of war which are generally kept separate: its intellectual history, its political and strategic dimensions, its social and cultural underpinnings, without forgetting the experiences of ordinary combatants. Finally, and in a stark challenge to our common sensibilities, Bell argues that total war sprang not out of the French Revolution's Republican ideology or its nationalism, but its irenic

RIGHT
David's famous painting of Napoelon crossing the Alps on his horse Marengo, circa 1801

yearning for absolute peace: the early 1790s saw France declare war on monarchical despotism in the very name of the ideals of peace and liberty – the precursor of the First World War's aspiration "to end all wars". This exterminationist logic, Bell claims, pushed the Revolution into an increasingly belligerent posture abroad. It also provoked a savage internal conflict at home against all manifestations of "counter-Revolution", which culminated in the killing fields of the Vendée, where at least 250,000 men, women and children died in 1793–4. One of the perpetrators of this butchery, General Turreau, is still honoured on the Arc de Triomphe.

Napoleon Bonaparte represented the apogee of this new warrior culture. Bell draws an arresting picture of the rise to power of this charismatic Revolutionary general, and shows how his seizure of power in 1799 represented the logical culmination of the militarization of the Revolution. Bonaparte's regime instituted an unprecedented cult of the military: 97 per cent of all those decorated with the Legion d'Honneur were from the armed forces. Indeed the

Grande Armée was held up as the embodiment of civic virtue, and its leader's power rested on an original cult, which all at once celebrated his "popular" origins and legitimacy, but also his martial prowess and his quasi-divine status; the ever-obliging Vatican even canonized a saint in his honour.

In his analysis of Napoleon's early military triumphs at Ulm, Austerlitz and Jena, as well as in his later setbacks in Spain and Russia, Bell emphasizes the growing pervasiveness of the culture of total war: the exponential growth of combatant forces (while 60,000 men had fought at Marengo in 1800, 500,000 combatants took part in the Battle of Leipzig, which was also grandly known as the Battle of the Nations, in 1813); the demonization not only of enemy forces but also of entire peoples; and the extreme excesses of partisan war in Italy and Spain, which severely crippled French forces and provoked savage reprisals against civilians, chillingly anticipating the bestiality of Nazi behaviour in parts of Occupied Europe. Bell insists on the absolute primacy of this new war culture: Napoleon appears not only as its progenitor but also as its instrument, and later as its victim.

Trapped by the inexorable logic of total war, the French Emperor lurched into ever more desperate military and political gambles, until the final debacle at Waterloo in 1815.

Yet as Karma Nabulsi's *Traditions of War* (1999) reminds us, Gustavus Adolphus carried a copy of Grotius's *De Jure Belli ac Pacis* (*On the Laws of War and Peace*) in his saddlebag as he laid waste the territories he conquered. And Bell himself shows that many of the key participants in the debates of the early 1790s were arguing tactically rather than out of genuine ideological conviction: Mirabeau, for example, proposed to codify the renunciation of expansionary war, even though he did not believe it; while Robespierre was at

"

The Grande Armée was seen by many as a liberating force in the countries it penetrated

SUDHIR HAZAREESINGH

ABOVE
An anonymous artist's impression of the Battle of Waterloo, June 18, 1815

this time an ardent opponent of war and political violence (as we know, he moved on quickly to better things). If Napoleon was so ghastly to his Army, too, why did his soldiers endure such sufferings across his campaigns, take such insane risks in battle, and worship his memory with such fervour after 1815? There is little evidence, furthermore, that the rhetoric of absolute enmity was actually internalized by the European populations of the time; and there are clear indications to the contrary – not least the fact that many French soldiers stayed on and made their homes in Russia after Napoleon's retreat in 1812 (imagine officers from the Waffen SS trying to settle in the Dordogne in 1945). The Grande Armée was seen by many as a liberating force in the countries it penetrated; to this day Napoleon is invoked in Poland's national anthem. In fact, he was reinvented as a constitutional liberal, the progenitor of Republicanism, the symbol of meritocracy and individualism, and the father of European unity – and it is this rosy, comforting myth which successive generations have celebrated up to this day. ∎

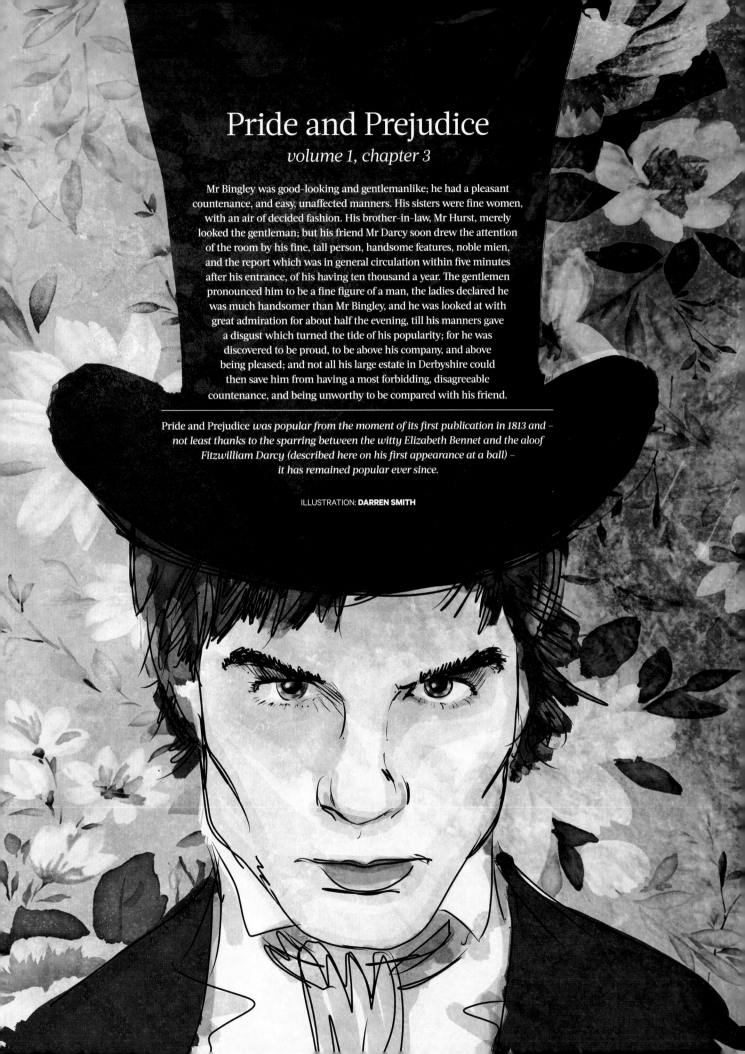

Pride and Prejudice
volume 1, chapter 3

Mr Bingley was good-looking and gentlemanlike; he had a pleasant countenance, and easy, unaffected manners. His sisters were fine women, with an air of decided fashion. His brother-in-law, Mr Hurst, merely looked the gentleman; but his friend Mr Darcy soon drew the attention of the room by his fine, tall person, handsome features, noble mien, and the report which was in general circulation within five minutes after his entrance, of his having ten thousand a year. The gentlemen pronounced him to be a fine figure of a man, the ladies declared he was much handsomer than Mr Bingley, and he was looked at with great admiration for about half the evening, till his manners gave a disgust which turned the tide of his popularity; for he was discovered to be proud, to be above his company, and above being pleased; and not all his large estate in Derbyshire could then save him from having a most forbidding, disagreeable countenance, and being unworthy to be compared with his friend.

Pride and Prejudice *was popular from the moment of its first publication in 1813 and – not least thanks to the sparring between the witty Elizabeth Bennet and the aloof Fitzwilliam Darcy (described here on his first appearance at a ball) – it has remained popular ever since.*

ILLUSTRATION: **DARREN SMITH**

The Afterlife

THE AFTERLIFE

Praise and pewter

How the Austen family fought over their most famous
member's legacy – and how Jane Austen herself sought after fame

AUTHOR: **CLAUDIA L. JOHNSON**

Lord Iddesleigh observed in 1900 that Janeites are equally eager to read Jane Austen and read about her: "it would be a very delightful thing", he wrote, "if a magazine could be started which should be devoted entirely to Miss Austen . . . . We are never tired of talking about her; should we ever grow weary of reading or writing about her?". Henry James looked on the publication of books by and about Austen during the late nineteenth and early twentieth centuries as an irredeemably commercial affair. In 1905, he censured the "special bookselling spirit" which, with all its "eager, active interfering force" (rather like a nautical Mrs Norris), whipped up a "stiff breeze" that drove the waters of Austen's reputation above their natural levels. For Iddesleigh the profusion of books seemed instead to signify a marvellous plenitude, serving a literary pleasure that, miraculously, never palls.

Claire Harman begins *Jane's Fame* (2009) by showing that many relatives and neighbours in the Austen circle – Egerton Brydges, James Henry Leigh, Mary Leigh, Cassandra Cooke and

BELOW
Jennifer Ehle as
Elizabeth Bennet in
the BBC adaptation
of *Pride and
Prejudice,* 1995

Austen's eldest brother James – were or aspired to be writers, and that having literary ambitions was not particularly remarkable. From her early teens onwards, when she made a practice of signing her dedications "THE AUTHOR", Austen knew who and what she was, and unlike Frances Burney, who concealed her authorship from her father, she wrote and published novels with the encouragement of her immediate family. Harman invites us to conceive of Austen both as a dedicated writer and also as a "hard-nosed" one. Thus she stresses Austen's umbrage over the non-appearance of *Susan* (later *Northanger Abbey*), which Benjamin Crosby bought in 1803 and even advertised but never saw fit to publish; her irritation that Walter Scott's (unsigned) review of *Emma* in *Quarterly Review* (March 1816) neglected to mention *Mansfield Park*; her worry, expressed in a letter of 1816, that she might soon "over-write" herself. Harman's Austen, by contrast, enjoys fame as well as profit. "I like praise as well as anybody", she wrote in 1814, with bracing directness, "I like what Edward calls Pewter too." In Mary

Russell Mitford's description of Austen's progress, from a "perpendicular, precise, taciturn piece of single-blessedness" as unregarded as "a poker or a firescreen" to "a poker of whom every one is afraid", Harman discerns not merely an anxiety on the part of others that their frailties or fatuity might end up immortalized in her novels, but a decision on Austen's part about how to conduct the power her fame conferred on her as a published writer, a decision to be "actively unpleasant" rather than make them feel at ease. To go from Harman's "active unpleasantness" to D. W. Harding's "regulated hatred" requires perhaps a few steps, but while the astringency of Harding's Austen is in the service of a fundamentally critical social vision – she would not "have helped to make her society what it was, or ours what it is" – the aloofness of Harman's Austen has smaller stakes, designed to keep people at a distance.

As the Austen scholar Kathryn Sutherland has shown, and as collateral descendants today freely attest, different branches of the Austen family jockeyed for place as privileged witnesses to, and

keepers of, Austen's legacy during the nineteenth century. The Hampshire Austens – James Edward Austen-Leigh, in particular – celebrated a somewhat homespun and domestic figure, but to the wealthier Kentish branch – represented in particular by Fanny Knight Knatchbull (the daughter of Edward Austen Knight, and Austen's favourite niece) and her son Lord Brabourne, who edited the first collection of Austen's letters – Austen was decidedly *déclassée*. Fanny Knight Knatchbull infamously described "Aunt Jane" as "not so refined as she ought to have been": "both Aunts (Cassandra & Jane) were brought up in the most complete ignorance of the World & its ways (I mean as to fashion & c)". As Fanny would have it, Jane and Cassandra would have been entirely "common", were it not for the improving company of her affluent, refined parents.

Although Fanny's remarks have not exactly been repressed – biographers and commentators have continued to produce them from time to time – they are generally treated as evidence either of senility or of an apostasy so nasty as

to be best left unnoticed, and as a result they have never made a dent in the myth of Austenian family love and solidarity. We can only imagine that Fanny here is, at least in part, repeating the sort of remarks her parents made about their talented but under-bred sister. And, as Harman shows, even the relentlessly idealizing James Edward Austen-Leigh goes out of his way to present Austen and her family as exemplars of a different, simpler and more frugal historical period – take, for example, the fact that the Austens grew their own potatoes – thus "head[ing] off any misjudgment of the family as vulgar or poor".

Was Austen rustic? Might Austen's wealthy brother have viewed her and Cassandra the way the contemptibly venal John Dashwood views his impoverished sisters, Elinor and Marianne, in *Sense and Sensibility* – and the way Elinor and Marianne in turn view the vulgar Steele sisters? And what might it say about Austen that she would recast family tensions in this way? Fanny's remarks at least suggest that not everyone in Austen's family treasured her talent and her fame as

ABOVE
Jane Austen Festival
in Bath, 2016

much as Cassandra or Henry did, and that authorship carried no particular status for the Godmersham relations, who likely regarded her much as Lady Middleton did the Dashwood sisters: "because they were fond of reading, she fancied them satirical: perhaps without exactly knowing what it was to be satirical; but that did not signify. It was censure in common use, and easily given".

Austen is today virtually equated with the Regency period, and for the world she has conquered, her time and our time have now collapsed into each other. Hence the ceaseless flow of Jane-inspired dramatizations on film, in print, the internet, and hence the photographs of the actress Olivia Williams playing Jane in the television film *Miss Austen Regrets* (2008) on sale at the Jane Austen Centre in Bath as if she were the real Jane Austen, or the pictures of the actor Colin Firth as Mr Darcy, as though he were the "real" Darcy. All of this would make Henry James recoil, but Iddlesleigh was right: we never tire of reading or writing about Austen, and all the ever-ramifying epiphenomena she generates do deliver. ∎

Austen adapted

Jane Austen's novels have frequently been dramatized for the big or small screen – although not always to be the best effect, as the *TLS*'s critics can testify

Northanger Abbey, 1986

In the Stock Exchange of literary reputations Jane Austen is a blue chip name. Dickens may fluctuate as Galsworthy tumbles and Aphra Behn soars, but Austen remains as solid an investment as Coca Cola or Levi's jeans. Like other brand leaders, however, her stock is subject to counterfeits, and this latest *Northanger Abbey* seems in serious danger from the Trades Descriptions Act. Maggie Wadey's adaptation is described as being "from the novel by Jane Austen": "from" is a very modest word to use.

"Purists", boasts the *Radio Times*, "will not be happy" with the liberties which the film has taken with the book. For, though the events and characters remain more or less in place, they are so modernized in idiom and style that the film's period details seem like props in an elaborate fancy-dress party. What is entirely missing is the light but serious tone of ridicule, the voice of reason at play. From first to last Jane Austen's narrative is witty, detached, ironic, but the ninety-minute film lacks any such controlling voice or tone. Its continuities are supplied by Ilona Sekacz's musical

score, which ranges from saxophone blues to sepulchral monkish chants, and by a visual style of seductive spectacle and overt sensuality. Shot largely in close-up, the film replaces Austen's conversation-piece style with a succession of dialogues of meaningful glances. Katherine Schlesinger as Catherine Morland acts mainly with her eyes, casting moony, soulful glances at all she meets. Peter Firth as Henry Tilney and Jonathan Coy as John Thorpe are equally fluent, employing a full vocabulary of ogles, leers, lascivious glances and knowing stares which reinforce the verbal innuendoes of a script which labours to make Jane Austen sexy. When General Tilney (Robert Hardy) commends Catherine on "the charming elasticity of your walk" his words, and accompanying leer, have a lubricity quite absent from the narrator's use of a similar phrase in the novel. Isabella's worldly remark, "You know how it is with men. They take no denial", is delivered with a lip-smacking eroticism. Cassie Stuart plays Isabella as a flouncing, bouncing flirt with a heaving bosom and a rolling eye, who seems to have tumbled straight from the

pages of *Moll Flanders* or *Fanny Hill*. The Tilney brothers snort snuff (we are never told that Henry is a clergyman), and among the bizarre inhabitants of the Abbey is a black-clad marchioness in death's-head make-up.

Producers and directors may sometimes despair of pleasing their critics when it comes to televising literary classics. If they play safe they are accused of an O level literal-mindedness, while if they attempt, as here, to reinterpret the work in cinematic terms they run into the charge of travesty. It should be said then that this is no crude or routine piece of vulgarization but an ambitious failure, an enterprising and often highly polished attempt to produce a *Northanger Abbey* for our times. The director Giles Foster has evidently tried to establish cinematic parallels for the delicious frisson of fear which Anne Radcliffe's gothic fictions inspired in Catherine Morland's teenage imagination. His solution, using imagery drawn from Hammer horror films and from Mills and Boon romance, deliberately exploits the status of both as clichés to inveigle viewers into a

self-conscious identification with Catherine's adolescent fantasies. It is a device which, used with greater tact and control, might well have succeeded, but merged into the film's overall seductive sensuality these images lose their ironic force, becoming part of a larger romantic fantasy. This persists until the end, when Peter Firth looms out of the mists on his white horse to sweep Catherine into his arms for a final lingering kiss.

The film has some marvellous visual moments which almost compensate, in their opulence, for its lack of structural coherence. The tea party in the Roman bath at Bath is a scene worthy of Fellini, with ladies, in bonnets piled high with ostrich feathers, exchanging polite conversation while immersed to the breasts in the steaming waters. Indeed hats provide the film's nearest equivalent to wit. Googie Withers plays Mrs Allen as a Regency Edna Everage with a new hat for every scene. Turbans and coifs, broad-brims and bonnets sprout from her head like exotic blooms. It is only a pity that the script shows more confidence in millinery than in irony.

DAVID NOKES

Sense and Sensibility, 1995

The most striking thing about Ang Lee's very enjoyable film of *Sense and Sensibility* is the way it has seized a complex, rather introverted novel and turned it into a major motion picture. It opens with Mr Dashwood gasping on his deathbed and closes with a country wedding, all ribbons and village children and bridal wreaths. In between, everything goes on at a swift pace; gentlemen gallop to and fro; carriages rattle across barren heathland; suitors are ushered in and out; reputations are threatened and hearts lost with the utmost dispatch. It could hardly be more different from the even-paced, television-serial Jane Austen we are used to - even the BBC's recent *plein-air Pride and Prejudice* did not quite have this brio. Boldness is the outstanding feature of Emma Thompson's screenplay, which simplifies plot, cuts characters and invents new scenes, some of them very broadly based. The narrative is opened out at every point; a single Austenian sentence is turned into dialogue, close-ups and significant

LEFT
A tea party in the Roman bath at Bath, in *Northanger Abbey*, 1986

looks. Life at Norland Park is rich cinema. The pianoforte is played in half-empty Regency rooms; Marianne attempts to find out Elinor's feelings with the full complement of curl-papers, candlestick and goffered nightgown; Elinor visits the servants' hall, a picturesque sea of white aprons and mob caps; the ball at which Marianne confronts Willoughby is crowded with glittering extras forming quadrilles. Life at Barton Cottage is poor cinema - a series of charming domestic vignettes of sewing, account books, lessons, picnics. The scenery shows the empty skies and wooded slopes of an eighteenth-century England. Lavish use is made of dogs, horses, woolly sheep and crying babies.

Lee's slight naivety of approach helps to create comedy. He has clearly taken to heart the novel's notion of "the ridicule so justly annexed to sensibility".

The early scenes, in particular, are full of a sort of rollicking humour in which the wickedness of Fanny (Harriet Walter as a modern-day Margaret Lockwood), the awkwardness of

Edward (Hugh Grant with hunched shoulders and a baffled expression) and the romantic excesses of Marianne and Willoughby (Kate Winslet and Greg Wise) are manifestly absurd. Everything is slightly exaggerated. Marianne is carried through the pouring rain not once but twice; Edward is faced with a brace of fiancées, who both cherish a handkerchief with the initials E. C. F.; and there is a happy moment when Elinor is left holding an unwanted cup of tea, as from behind three different bedroom doors there comes the sound of hearty weeping. In minor roles, there are some splendidly ripe performances from Robert Hardy (as Sir John Middleton), Elizabeth Spriggs (Mrs

Lavish use is made of dogs, horses, woolly sheep and crying babies

LINDSAY DUGUID

Jennings) and Hugh Laurie (Mr Palmer).

Instead of disappearing under this treatment, the themes of the novel stand out clearly. The men may have the country mansions and the horses, but the women have the interesting emotional lives. We see the state of anxious anticipation to which Elinor and Marianne are condemned, awaiting the knock on the door, the announcement of the visitor or the arrival of a letter in a fever of reined-in agitation. They are constantly overset with disappointment when the right man does not come; it is Colonel Brandon when it ought to be Willoughby, and Edward when he is least expected. Throughout, there lurks the threat of the dreadful fate of the outcast female, in the tragedy of Colonel Brandon's poor Eliza and her bastard daughter - "ruination and despair", seclusion from society, poverty and death. Who can blame Lucy Steele for her sly, tenacious grip on the Ferrars family, or Mrs Jennings for her shaming references to the need to get married. Thompson's script provides a substantial part and a symbolic function

ABOVE
Clockwise from top-left: Greg Wise as John Willoughby and Kate Winslet as Marianne Dashwood; Kate Winslet, Emilie François as Margaret Dashwood and Emma Thompson as Elinor Dashwood; Kate Winslet, Emma Thompson and film crew, *Sense and Sensibility*, 1995

for the third Dashwood sister (played with ingenuous energy by thirteen-year-old Emilie François) who, fascinated by her sisters' love affairs, is still learning not to say the right thing on the wrong occasion. Her future is the focus for all the conversations about how to behave.

The novel's social observation is honoured. Edward, Willoughby and Colonel Brandon all take Marianne's verse-reading test, putting expression into stanzas by Cowper and Hartley Coleridge, though success in this turns out to be misleading. The unworthy characters (Fanny, Willoughby, Robert Ferrars) all speak in praise of cottages, as if they could, by mere money, attain the domestic harmony of Barton Cottage. The importance of income is continually stated; the actual amount of every dowry, legacy and fortune is whispered from mouth to mouth; the opening event is the whittling down of the Dashwoods' inheritance; the closing image a handful of coins thrown in the air by Colonel Brandon on his wedding day.

The final success of the film, however, is not in the detail but in the way it sustains an atmosphere of intense feeling, a romantic responsiveness to human affection; the emotional high point of the final proposal (when Emma Thompson manages a chilling fit of hysterical weeping on the realization that Edward is free to marry) is challenged by Marianne's fever at Cleveland Park, an affecting episode, with the local doctor talking of laudanum, bleeding the patient into a china bowl and looking grave. It seems all too likely that the girl will die at the age of sixteen. Elinor's plea to her sister, "Do not leave me alone" is very moving - a demonstration of pure sensibility in its proper place.

LINDSAY DUGUID

Bride And Prejudice, 2004

Gurinder Chadha's *Bride and Prejudice* has the kind of bare-faced cheek that is likely to delight and disgust Janeites in equal measures. Admittedly, with such disparate commentators as Salman Rushdie and James Wood united in noting Austen's relevance to (and possible influence on) Indian writing in English, it takes only a small leap of imagination to re-imagine the story of Elizabeth and Darcy as a full-blown, cross-cultural Bollywood musical; then again, Chadha's film, as an Austen spin-off, may have more to live up to.

Clueless (1995), Amy Heckerling's extraordinary relocation of *Emma* to contemporary Beverly Hills, set the benchmark for "free" literary adaptations. It worked so well that Douglas McGrath's "straight" cinema version, released the following year, felt less close to the original novel, despite its more dutiful heritage-movie values and a finely judged lead performance from Gwyneth Paltrow. One of *Bride and Prejudice*'s strongest suits, therefore, is the ease with which Austen's central plot appears to fit into its new locations, with Amritsar, London and Los Angeles taking the places of Longbourn, Netherfield and Pemberley – a circumstance which opens up once more the vexed question of accuracy versus fidelity, the letter and the spirit, in matters of screen transposition.

For every aspect of *Pride and Prejudice* that Chadha and her co-writer Paul Mayeda Berges use with minimum alteration (Lady Lucas's "triumph on being able to retort on Mrs Bennet the comfort of having a daughter well married"), there are others that require more careful consideration, or tactful omission. For example, Darcy's saying "She is tolerable" of the Bollywood superstar and former Miss World, Aishwarya Rai,

would have elicited the wrong kind of laughter. Perhaps most ingenious of all the changes is the decision to turn Darcy (Martin Henderson) into an all-American hotelier. What in Austen's original are matters of monetary incompatibility begin, here, to shade into matters of cultural difference, with Darcy and Lalita/Elizabeth falling out over the former's attempts to package India as an "exotic" tourist location.

Of course, viewers coming to *Bride and Prejudice* expecting what Austen described to her sister Cassandra as the "playfulness and epigrammatism" of the novel's "general style" are likely to be disappointed. One reason why *Clueless* remains unsurpassed in this modern genre is that Heckerling's film found in the "whatever"-speak of Californian teenagers a slang capable of conveying something of *Emma*'s atmosphere of deception and covert emotion. In comparison, some of *Bride and Prejudice*'s dialogue rather clunks along, and Henderson and Rai seem much happier tearing strips off each other in the early scenes than they are when caressing conversationally near the end.

But Bollywood movies are not only about dialogue, and Chadha has a useful ally in her cinematographer, Santosh Sivan, himself the director of the Shah Rukh Khan historical epic *Asoka*. The excellently shot social dance sequences

ABOVE
Peeya Rai Choudhuri as Lakhi Bakshi, Aishwarya Rai as Lalita Bakshi and Namrata Shirodkar as Jaya Bakshi Balraj in *Bride and Prejudice*, 2004

that stand in for the original's ballrooms often capture the novel's coded flirtations and "civil disdain" better than the dialogue, and Chadha and Sivan stage numerous loving parodies of Bollywood cinematic conventions, not least the gleefully corny establishing shots (the Hollywood sign, the London Eye) – although Chadha's London is a masterpiece of Loach-and-Leigh grit compared to that portrayed in blockbusters such as *Kabhi Khushi Khabhie Gham* (2001). There is even a sly nod at Bollywood's irrational location changes, when Darcy and Lalita, who confess their love in Los Angeles, are suddenly pictured in what appears to be the courtyard of Somerset House, with Darcy's wet shirt presumably a further allusion to Colin Firth's emergence from a lake in the BBC's adaptation eight years ago.

Bride and Prejudice, too, avoids the darker undercurrents of Austen, but then it never pretends to be anything other than a relentlessly upbeat comedy, a kind of Four Weddings and No Funerals; and while it never attains the heights of *Clueless*, it is at least far from clueless itself. Any adaptation is bound to be selective, and for all its flaws, Chadha's film at least provides a new slant on what Austen identified as the "light, and bright, and sparkling" side of her novel. No life without wife, indeed.

BHARAT TANDON

Persuasion, 1995

The standard opening shot of classic novel adaptations - the carriage clopping through the lanes to the forecourt of the great house - is intercut in the Screen Two film, *Jane Austen's Persuasion* (*sic*), with stirring visions of men-of-war at anchor. But the immediate associations of domestic grandeur and perilous adventure are quickly overturned. For the carriage brings to the door of the spendthrift Baronet, Sir Walter Elliot, the agent who is arranging the letting of the ancestral home to an Admiral returning wealthy from the wars and the household's humiliating removal to Bath.

Sir Walter's middle daughter, Anne, is said to be versed in "the art of knowing our own nothingness beyond our own sphere"; but she is next to nothing at home as well, and her one prospect of fulfilment - Captain Wentworth, whom she rejected eight years previously on well-meant but wrongly grounded advice - has since been busily something all over the globe. Caught between two self-important sisters, this fading Cinderella has become an unconsidered support to the vanity of others, playing the piano for their ridiculous dance.

Her only protest in the novel is through the mildest strand of her creator's irony ("Captain Benwick was not inconsolable. That was a point which Anne had not been able to avoid

> *The strips, the lime greens and oranges, the ubiquitous shock of* yellow, *make it feel like Zanzibar*

MICK IMLAH

suspecting before"); and when Wentworth returns to her sphere, her nature and her circumstances decree that there is nothing she can do to accelerate the gradations of hope he begins to offer.

Such a private and passive heroine - one temperamentally unable to make a scene - is awkward to dramatize; and *Persuasion* has only once been filmed before. The casting of Amanda Root, whose big eyes have a silent-movie expressiveness, is a good start; and the adaptor, Nick Dear, has employed a fair blend of resourcefulness and roughness in his treatment. (It's *not* his fault that the single scene of violent action, Louisa Musgrove's fall at Lyme, is as poorly realized here as it is in the novel: the only point where the use of slow motion - is certainly not appropriate). Resource is apparent in the early montage in which Anne hears the complaints of each of the Musgrove family in turn about the others, culminating in her brother-in-law's exasperated, slumping exclamation, "Oh, Anne!" - a nice little invention. But you can only prod a suffering silence in so many ways, and it is as well when Wentworth (Ciaran Hinds) arrives to handsomely intensify it.

None the less, the business between the lovers - the look here, the helping hand there, the flash of jealousy so much later that provokes such minutely detailed sensations in the book - may need to be made more explicit for film; and there is some sacrifice involved. When Wentworth leaves a concert in Bath, because he misunderstands Anne's patience with an eligible suitor, she tries to detain him with as much boldness as she could ever muster: "Is not this song worth staying for?" Instead, Dear has her frothing that "the next song is very beautiful it's a very beautiful *love* song", and dancing around him in a tizzy; where she has

patently ceased to be the old Anne Elliot who now resignedly returns to her seat.

That they are finally made to kiss in the streets of Bath - surrounded, what's more, by an Italian circus procession arouses ambivalent feelings: that this transgresses the novel's prescription of "smiles reined in and spirits dancing in private rapture"; that it rudely forsakes the real constraints of Jane Austen's world for the high seas of passion; but that it is something that women in Anne Elliot's position, in Jane Austen's position, may have been dying to do.

It should also be said that, in optical terms, the film (or more especially the fantastic costumes) offers the viewer an escape too, through the sense that this constructed past really is another country: even if the turbans, the skull caps, the stripes, the lime greens and oranges, the ubiquitous shock of *yellow*, make it feel like Zanzibar.

MICK IMLAH

Mansfield Park, 1999

Today it is largely television and movie adaptations that produce and circulate fantasies about Austenian elegance. As these productions have become a phenomenon, they have inflated cosiness into opulence; costumes have become too lavish, gentlemen too strapping, country houses too grandiose, and all too idealized, too much. But while we make a fetish of furniture and dress in these adaptations, it would be wise to remember that Austen's novels are indifferent to this kind of specificity.

There has always been another, less conspicuous, vision of Austen and her work. This other Austen is seen as alienated from the world that prettifies her, an Austen whom D. W. Harding celebrated for her "regulated hatred" and for her refusal to help "make her society what it was, or ours what it is". The iconoclastic Austen is beloved not for the primness, propriety, or romantic conventionality imputed to her, but for the energy of her satire, for the irreverence and, to some, even the bitchiness of her wit, for the trenchant nature of her social criticism, and the complexity of her characters' passions – passions sharpened by intelligence and intensified by good manners.

Readers attached to the dissenting Austen will enjoy the new *Mansfield Park*, directed and written by Patricia Rozema (*I've Heard the Mermaids Singing*, *When Night Is Falling*). Rozema's *Mansfield Park* is a stunning revisionist reading of Austen's darkest novel. Adaptations cannot replicate the novel on which they are based, and Rozema's movie, more of an intervention than an adaptation, departs radically and frequently. Despite paying lip-service to civility, Janeites tend to be the grumpiest of fans, and many have taken umbrage at Rozema's deviations. More than simple purism is

at issue here: Austen's own narrative method makes us feel so uniquely privileged in our closeness to her that we readily believe that no one could possibly understand or visualize a character as perfectly as we alone can, and in all decency – decency, mind you – should not even try. For true believers, adaptations will not only disappoint but scandalize. Yet Rozema's "unfaithfulness" obliges us to think responsibly about what we want a director to be faithful to. I am unfazed by changes to the plot or gaffes in costuming and manners – the ante-bellum gowns of the 1940 *Pride and Prejudice*, for example. But when free indirect discourse is changed into voice-over, I cringe in agony, and when the first sentence of *Pride and Prejudice* becomes a piece of dialogue, I stop watching. On these counts, Rozema's film is faithful, for it gives us what many of us love about Austen in the first place, what other movies never deliver: Austen's presence as a narrator.

Rozema accomplishes this fidelity by unapologetic infidelity in another respect. Instead of the frail, self-denying, inhibited girl of the novel, Rozema's Fanny Price is sturdy, energetic, and self-possessed. In her very abjection, Austen's heroine is fascinating. It was jolting to encounter Rozema's change, and hard to stop regretting it. But once I did, I found the innovation ingenious and rewarding, conducing towards the last thing we expect from Austen-iana nowadays, alas: freshness and surprise. Here, Fanny retreats to her room not to struggle with feelings of injury, but to engage in the sweetest revenge: writing well. She scribbles the raucous stories Austen wrote when she was a girl – "Henry and Eliza", for example, in which the heroine finds herself imprisoned, her two fingers bitten off and devoured by her hungry children;

RIGHT
Jonny Lee Miller as Edmund Bertram and Frances O'Connor as Fanny Price in *Mansfield Park*, 1999

and "The History of England", in which Fanny (thinking of her snooty relations?) observes of the "row" Joan of Arc caused among the English, "They should not have burnt her but they did". By weaving in Austen's uproarious early writings, Rozema transforms Fanny into a version of the Austenian narrator we love. In the process, she gets across the novel's funniness – no small feat – for as a writing-heroine, Fanny, likeably played by Frances O'Connor, takes over the narrator's acerbic lines, as when she describes Maria Bertram's wedding with the quip, "her mother stood with salts in her hand, expecting to be agitated, and her aunt tried to cry".

But this spirited heroine with a flair for comedy encounters a history of England that is not funny. Small wonder no one has been standing in line to film *Mansfield Park*: the earnest clergyman, the dignified father, the vivacious young lady, the dashing young man, even the good girl are all benighted, and their country house tainted. To discover why, we must address what some read Austen to avoid: politics. In a haunting early scene, torn from her family to be treated as a semi-menial among affluent relations, Fanny hears a wailing song from a ship off the coast. "Black cargo", the coachman says. The comforts of Fanny's new home, we learn, come from slave labour on plantations owned by Fanny's uncle, Sir Thomas. Drawing on Austen's attachment to abolitionist

Rozema doesn't glamorize the country estate, and this is one of her most transgressive moves

CLAUDIA L. JOHNSON

writers, Rozema doesn't glamorize the country estate, and this is one of her most transgressive moves. Her cinematographer is Michael Coulter, who also shot Lee's *Sense and Sensibility*, with its lustrous blues and its penchant for the spectacularly sumptuous.

Filmed at Kirby Hall, which is not inhabited, the country house in *Mansfield Park*, by contrast, is shot mostly in cream and yellow tones, and it looks cold, at times scarcely furnished, and in disrepair, corrupted by the moral crime on which it subsists and on which account it cannot thrive. In a climactic scene of Rozema's invention, Fanny discovers sketches depicting the torture and rape of Sir Thomas's slaves. These are not the pretty pictures we associate with Austen, and because of them the movie almost got an R-rating – a mind-boggling yet satisfying thought. But Austen, and most writers at the time, would have concurred in the moral if not the manner: Sir Thomas's misrule abroad

sullies his authority and leads to moral turpitude at home. Spurred on by the searing power of Harold Pinter's Sir Thomas, Rozema is unrelenting on this point.

Austen's Mansfield Park is a seductive place, and her Sir Thomas believes in his own show of benevolence. Pinter's Sir Thomas, depraved by unchecked power, makes no attempt even to appear right-thinking. Likewise, while it was a stroke of genius to cast Lindsay Duncan as both Mrs Price and Lady Bertram, temperamentally similar sisters separated by the gulf of class, it wasn't necessary to provide Lady Bertram, who exists in a stupor of native apathy shocking enough, with laudanum to boot.

Set on a course of radical criticism, Rozema emphasizes and augments the unseemliness unquestionably present in the novel, and only at the end of the film does she let up. Her movie is most arresting in its evocations of sexuality. On this subject, many readers and

viewers who are usually intelligent become stupid and priggish, as if it is indecent – indecent, mind you – to discover sexuality in Austen's novels, and as if the sexuality that is clearly there cannot possibly be sexuality. Scores of viewers who gasped with pleasure at a glimpse of Colin Firth's extra-textual derriere in the BBC's *Pride and Prejudice* denounce Rozema's movie on the grounds that there's no sex in Jane Austen, a conviction egregiously inapt with respect to *Mansfield Park*, which is suffused with frustrated, illicit, wayward, or polymorphous sexuality.

Finally, a director has taken risks with Austen, treating her work not as a museum piece or as a sacred text but as a living presence whose power inspires flight. *Mansfield Park* is an audaciously perceptive cinematic evocation of Austen's unblinking, yet forgiving vision, and an accomplishment of dazzling imagination and originality in its own right.

CLAUDIA L. JOHNSON

Clueless, 1995

Nothing dates as quickly as modernity. When *Clueless* was first released in 1995, writer/director Amy Heckerling's updating of Austen's *Emma* seemed like a brightly lit window into the future. The technology on display was brand-new; the clothes were fresh from the catwalk. Watching it again now, as teenagers take selfies with a 35mm camera or clamp brick-like mobile phones to their ears, is more like peering through the glass of a museum case. Even some of the social attitudes now seem rather dusty, as one character announces that another boy is "a disco-dancing, Oscar Wilde-reading, Streisand ticket-holding friend of Dorothy".

What remains startlingly fresh is Heckerling's decision to relocate the action to a Beverly Hills high school, an environment bound by social conventions that are no less rigid than those of Austen's Highbury. The teenagers may gather around lunch tables rather than card tables, and they may adopt different costumes to identify their particular social set (bum-hanging trousers for skaters; long hair and check shirts for slackers), but here too you're either a winner or a loser in the social stakes; either you're hot or you're not.

At the top of the pecking order is Cher (Alicia Silverstone), a beautiful sixteen-year-old who, like Austen's heroine, has "a comfortable home and a happy disposition". Also like Emma, she decides to take on a social inferior as her special project – in this case a sexually aware but socially gauche student named Tai (Brittany Murphy), who is swiftly given a makeover that allows her to blend into the fashionable crowd. Cher's Mr Knightley is her older stepbrother Josh (Paul Rudd), a college student whose intellectual credentials are indicated by the fact that he reads Nietzsche and is growing a goatee. He

quickly dismisses Cher as "a superficial space cadet" who belongs in the shopping mall rather than the library.

Yet one of the cleverest tricks this film plays is to make you realize that although Cher is as sweet as bubblegum, she is far from stupid. In between her bursts of "Whatever!" and "As if!", she casually drops words like "capricious" and "sporadic" into conversation. While she has only a hazy memory of some books (the conclusion of *A Tale of Two Cities*, she explains, is that "It is a far, far better thing doing stuff for other people"), she corrects one of Josh's friends who misattributes a line from *Hamlet*, and also alludes to Botticelli and Monet. She may be artless, but she knows her art. When the penny finally drops, and she realizes that all her bickering with Josh has really been an unwitting kind of flirting, their first kiss is more than just a meeting of lips. It also confirms a genuine meeting of minds.

Inevitably, the film trims away much that makes Austen's novel such a complicated delight to read. Whereas Mr Woodhouse is one of literature's great comic hypochondriacs, fearful of

ABOVE
Alicia Silverstone as Cher in *Clueless*, 1995

everything from draughts to undercooked asparagus, Cher's father is a tough-talking lawyer who refuses to drink his morning orange juice. The smooth young clergyman who proposes to *Emma* is transformed into Elton, a Beverley Hills brat with a sports car and wandering hands. Even the weather is simplified. In Austen it is a constant source of anxiety and a helpful generator of plot – it is because of a light snowfall that Emma finds herself trapped in a carriage with the drunk and amorous Mr Elton – but in the film it is as reliably sunny as Cher herself.

But although much is taken away, much remains. Several details of Austen's plot are given a sharp modern twist, like the relics from Harriet's encounters with Mr Elton (a plaster and a "bit of old pencil") that she hangs onto as "precious treasures", which in *Clueless* become a towel and a cassette of Coolio's 'Rollin' with my Homies', the song that – sigh – Tai danced to with the dishy Elton. There are also some sly in-jokes for the Janeites, as when Cher watches CNN and thinks that the Bosnian conflict is happening in the Middle East – a wink at the notion that

Austen was equally clueless about the Napoleonic Wars.

Most impressively, at times Heckerling discovers a cinematic equivalent for Austen's free indirect style, which allows us to see the world through Emma's eyes and at the same time notice what she seems to be missing. The scenes when Cher's shiny black phone fills the screen to the soundtrack of *2001: A space odyssey*, or Tai's red hair dye gurgles down the plughole like a benign outtake from *Psycho*, are more than just visual gags. They are little insights into the minds of teenagers for whom the line between real life and Hollywood has become a happy blur.

The result is a film that is, to borrow a phrase from one of Austen's letters, "light & bright & sparkling", albeit one that largely removes the irony rippling through that description. The final scene, at the wedding of two teachers Cher has brought together, includes a shot of some champagne glasses that the guests have been drinking from. It's a mark of the film's optimism that they look half-full rather than half-empty.

ROBERT DOUGLAS-FAIRHURST

Emma, 1996

There are moments to cherish in *Emma* – moments when the scriptwriters, struggling to express, in modern, accessible terms, the essence of a scene written 180 years ago, cast wildly about for a suitable idiom and achieve exquisite bathos. One comes early on in the film when Emma and Harriet Smith have tripped into a smoky cottage interior with a basket of good things. Emma gently asks the old lady how she does, and the crone quavers back with perfect sitcom timing, "Mustn't grumble". Another is Mr Knightley's proposal: "Marry me, my wzonderful, darling friend", he pleads, against a background of strings before closing in for the kiss.

The screenplay (by the film's director, Douglas McGrath) is the chief drawback to the latest Jane Austen. Mistrusting the original material and the intended audience, it flattens character, broadens comedy and simplifies plot. Mr Woodhouse, Miss Bates and Mrs Elton are simply the occasion for crude humour. The main thrust of the film is how Emma (a minx) and Harriet (a klutz) get their husbands, so that the complexities of Jane Fairfax's hidden engagement and the threat posed to Emma by Frank Churchill are much diminished; the mystery of the pianoforte is set up but never solved; the comings and goings at the Donwell Abbey picnic are ignored. In place of the book's mixture of conversation and interior monologue, there are elaborate flashbacks, soliloquies and voiceovers. Emma confides her feelings about Mr Knightley to Mrs Weston, prays aloud in a deserted chapel and even explains why she is writing with a quill pen in a bound volume: "Dear Diary . . . ."

Perhaps to compensate for the inadequate words, the screen is packed with movement; the streets of Highbury

are crammed with sheep and yokels; the gypsies who frighten Harriet are a small mob, intent on rape, who throw her to the ground; the formal dance at the Coles party goes on and on; Emma's joke at Miss Bates's expense falls cataclysmically flat (there is no question that it might be funny), whereupon Mr Knightley rants at her in a fury. Despite these intrusions, the tempo of the film is anxious, hurrying; there is much taking of dinner and tea, with characters seated at groaning tables, waving their food around, chewing energetically and talking with their mouths full. It seems almost impossible for them to talk naturally when the sentences are long or complex; faced with saying something like "Mr Knightley's air is so remarkably good that it is not fair to compare Mr Martin with him", the surreally dainty Gwyneth Paltrow emphasizes every cadence by raising her eyebrows, widening her eyes and pointing her chin. Even the more experienced members of the cast, such as Sophie Thompson and Alan Cumming, are driven to actorly excess. To overcome the awkwardness of speech, the characters are always busy with something – archery, catching butterflies, picking flowers, playing with puppies. The screen is filled with eye-catching splendour – orchards, rivers, gardens, drawing-rooms full of wall-paper and paintings – and lit with extravagant care, glowing with candlelight and firelight, dappled by the sun.

Regency England, with pelisses, its comfortable country seats and its roaming strangers, has long been the place for romance. Frances Burney invented it, Georgette Heyer capitalized on it, now Hollywood is exploiting it. That Jane Austen was doing something altogether different seems not to matter to the film-makers. *Emma* has found a new low in adaptations of her work.

LINDSAY DUGUID ■

THE AFTERLIFE

What would Jane Austen do?

The fine art of attending a Jane Austen conference – in Chicago

AUTHOR: **PAULA MARANTZ COHEN**

Picture this: several hundred people, many in Empire gowns, buttoned boots, and bonnets pirouetting in a stately line across a large ballroom. Women are partnering women for the most part, though here and there one sees a male specimen in knee breeches, long coat, and curled wig sashaying happily amid the beribboned throng.

The event is the Regency Ball of the Jane Austen Society of North America AGM, held at the Westin Hotel in Chicago in October, culminating in two days of total immersion in Austeniana. Preceding the ball was a gala banquet and costume parade down Chicago's Magnificent Mile. When the dancing ended, interested parties retired for games of whist at the little tables set up for the purpose in the lobby of the Westin.

This year marks the thirtieth anniversary of the Jane Austen Society of North America (JASNA), and the annual meeting featured a full range of festivity. Nothing raucous or vulgar, mind you, and only a few instances of untoward cleavage ("She would do well to sew a little lace over the bodice",

LEFT
Keira Knightley as Elizabeth Bennet and Matthew MacFadyen as Mr Darcy, in *Pride and Prejudice*, 2005

BELOW
Colin Firth as Mr Darcy, in *Pride and Prejudice*, 1995

one Austenite was overheard whispering to another regarding one plunging neckline).

Two full days were packed with special sessions on everything from textual cruxes in Austen novels to lessons in the dances of the Regency period. The titles of the talks ranged from the light-hearted ("Laughter over Tea: Jane Austen and culinary pedagogy") to the self-reflexive ("A Walk with Jane Austen: Seeing my life through Austen's lens"), to the pedagogical ("Introducing Austen to Military Students"), to the multicultural ("Austen's Legacy in Japan") – and on to such far-flung topics as "Jane Austen and Global Warming" and "Jane Austen's Legacy in Scent". There were also provocatively cryptic talks such as "Blogging Jane; or, Blog Snarkily and Carry a Big Cluebat" and "Mr Darcy is an Actor". The general title of this year's annual event was "Austen's Legacy: Life, Love and Laughter" – which pretty much covers everything, though with an eye to the Austen industry, which has been churning out spin-off books and movie adaptations at an amazing rate.

Some serious discussion was given

ABOVE
Regency Ball at the
Guildhall in Bath
organized by the
Jane Austen Festival

to the truth now universally acknowledged that many young people know Austen only by way of the BBC adaptations (with Mr Darcy inextricably linked with Colin Firth) or, worse, the Keira Knightley *Pride and Prejudice*, of the swirling music and full-mouthed kiss – so un-Austen-like in style and tone. On the other hand, say the less fundamentalist in the group, any route to Austen must be applauded. Even a movie "like that" could conceivably lead an impressionable young person to pick up the novel.

Jane Austen has always had her enthusiasts. F. R. Leavis and Lionel Trilling, arguably the most serious English-language critics of the twentieth century, both championed her genius. Trilling famously made a distinction between those who liked her for the right reasons and those who

liked her for the wrong ones.

In the former group he put people like himself, who saw Austen as the champion of an active and self-perfecting moral idyll. In the latter group, he placed the "gentle Jane-ites", those spinsterish types, well-meaning but vapid, who read her books for a cosy view of old England. This sort of division now seems condescending in the extreme. It suggests that Trilling, brilliant though he was, was not a close enough reader of Jane Austen, repeating, on a larger scale, Emma's insult to Miss Bates.

JASNA makes no such mistake. All are welcome and respected at the annual meeting. Intellectual rigour of the sort found, for example, in Peter Graham's book *Jane Austen & Charles Darwin: Naturalists and novelists* is presented side by side with "The Essential Regency

Bonnet Workshop (registration required)". And why not? Austen was both a moral heavyweight and a material girl. Her letters show her to have been partial to a nice bonnet. The pure pleasure of mixing the high and the low, the rigorous and the kitsch, the morally serious and the utterly frivolous make the JASNA AGM very different from the standard academic convention.

"What would Jane Austen do?" is a leitmotif – a question that one could do worse than pose in the midst of, say, fractious faculty meetings or presidential debates. The members of JASNA display a great deal of civility while engaging in copious talk, downing numerous cups of tea and imbibing, as day moves into evening and the card tables come out, not a few cocktails. Jane would certainly have approved. ∎

THE AFTERLIFE

Ostensibly Austen

Some of the many rewrites, spin-offs and sequels to Jane Austen's novels –
and what the *TLS*'s critics have made of them

Old Friends and New Fancies,
Sybil G. Brinton, 1913

"[*Old Friends and New Fancies*] by
Miss Brinton takes the original form of
continuing the fortunes of the characters
and devising marriages between them –
a work of great love and great ingenuity
which, if taken not as fiction but as
talk about Jane Austen's characters,
will please that select public which is
never tired of discussing them."
(Virginia Woolf)

Jane Fairfax,
Naomi Royde-Smith, 1940

"Of Jane Austen's novels *Emma* is the
severest test that novelist could set the
most adventurous and skilful worshipper
to follow. Miss Royde-Smith has the
courage, the skill and the equipment of
wide Austen-lore. In this novel she
undertakes to tell us more of Jane
Fairfax's story." (Anon)

Jane Austen in Australia,
Barbara Ker Wilson, 1984

"... we are given an enjoyable account of
early Australian life and an original view
of early nineteenth-century English
history. Despite occasional anachronisms

of expression *Jane Austen in Australia*
offers some rewarding contrasts;
incongruity is part of its appeal."
(Lindsay Duguid)

Mansfield Revisited,
Joan Aiken, 1984

"The scene-setting is not implausible, the
characters are not grotesquely wrong,
but we still feel affronted that *Mansfield
Park* should have been capitalized on in
this way." (Lindsay Duguid)

Mrs Rushworth,
Victor Gordon, 1989

"As a homage to a greater work,
Mrs Rushworth is more in the line of
Angela Thirkell than of Jean Rhys."
(Lindsay Duguid)

Pemberley,
Emma Tennant, 1993

"Emma Tennant's *Pemberley* attempts
that which Jane Austen never presumed:
to peer into the marital after-lives of her
characters ... this is accomplished by the
indefatigable reference to the 'prequel'
required to explain even the smallest of
nuances to those who have not read it –
a sensible show of dedication to possibly

BELOW
Renée Zellweger
in the 2001 film
of *Bridget Jones's
Diary*, adapted
from Helen
Fielding's novel

the only group of readers who will not be
offended by *Pemberley*." (Rachel Cusk)

Bridget Jones's Diary,
Helen Fielding, 1996

"One of the least attractive developments
in the current English press is the
proliferation of columns exposing the
details of the journalist's emotional and
domestic life .... It is extraordinary that
something with the lightness and vigour
of *Bridget Jones's Diary* could have
issued from under the screw of this crass
directive, but it has." (Nicola Shulman)

The Jane Austen Book Club,
Karen Joy Fowler, 2004

"... the book seems intentionally small
in scale and ambition. It is Jane Austen's
social microcosm reduced to an
even smaller microcosm."
(Paula Marantz Cohen)

The Watsons,
Merryn Williams, 2005

"The pleasure of reading Williams's
chapters ... comes only from the
satisfaction of completion, rather than
the rich pleasures derived from reading
Austen herself." (Sarah Savitt)

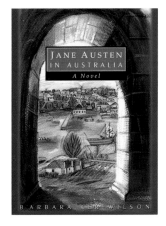

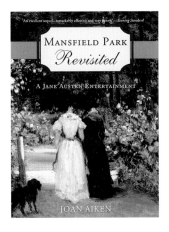

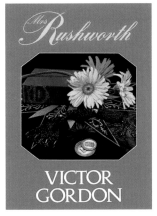

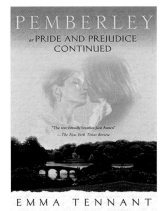

Mr Darcy's Diary,
Maya Slater, 2007

"Slater offers a new twist to the old formula. . . . [but] because *Mr Darcy's Diary* is fettered by its compulsion to annotate *Pride and Prejudice*, it is unable to take flight into a plausible fiction of its own." (Kathryn Sutherland)

Mary Bennet's Chance,
Virginia Aitken, 2011

"Aitken fails to find Austen's lightness of touch; she cannot match her material and moral thrift and the rich resonance of understatement . . . . However, Aitken rises well to the difficult challenge of the conversational voices . . . and the story unfolds with much relish and some skill." (Kathryn Sutherland)

Death Comes to Pemberley,
P. D. James, 2011

"The trouble with *Death Comes to Pemberley* is its writer's eagerness to crowd several different kinds of novel into a single narrative . . . . As a *jeu d'esprit* the book appears moderately diverting, but like so many other attempts at doing Jane it merely underlines the truth of her singularity." (Jonathan Keates) ■

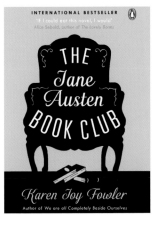

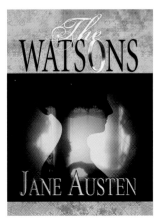

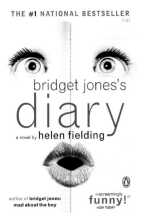

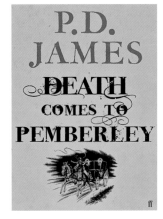

Persuasion

volume 2, chapter 4

"My idea of good company, Mr Elliot, is the company of clever, well-informed people, who have a great deal of conversation; that is what I call good company."
"You are mistaken", said he gently, "that is not good company, that is the best. Good company requires only birth, education and manners, and with regard to education is not very nice. Birth and good manners are essential; but a little learning is by no means a dangerous thing in good company, on the contrary, it will do very well.

In Anne Elliot, Austen created a heroine who encounters the man to whom she was once engaged, Captain Frederick Wentworth, seven years later. Persuasion is an autumnal, yet ultimately redemptive, last word.

ILLUSTRATION: **DARREN SMITH**